CHRISTINA M. CUMMINGS

The Journey Back to Self

A Beginner's Guide to Recovery from Cultic & Narcissistic Abuse

First published by Phoenix 33 Media 2025

First edition

ISBN: 979-8-9936412-0-1

Editing by Christina Houen

This book was professionally typeset on Reedsy.
Find out more at reedsy.com

To you, dear reader:

I wish you so well on your way. I wish you love and peace and purpose. For even if our paths never cross in person, I know that your healing journey is essential and it contributes to my own just as it does to every other soul walking this path with us. From the bottom of my heart, I thank you for the work that you have done, the work that you are doing and the work that you will yet do. Active, intentional healing is not for the faint of heart. This is warrior's work.

Contents

Introduction

How I Got Here

My last morning in the cult, I awoke before the sun rose. I'd barely slept the night before, dozing in and out of consciousness, a part of my mind perpetually on alert. I felt as if I could sense every nerve in my body firing electrical currents, and at the same time, I felt numb inside. Long term, extreme anxiety, resulting in persistent high-grade physical tension, lived in symbiosis with pure exhaustion and chronic dissociation. This had become my normal state of being somewhere over the last fourteen years. I was a numb live wire of exhausted tension that never stopped working, surviving and coping.

By the day I broke free, my mind, body and heart were all in tatters: I was a hot mess, to put it mildly. At forty-one years old, I dared to break the chains of cultic control, perhaps for the first time in my life. High-control and cultic coercion were all I had ever really known. Prior to the cult I landed in as an adult, I spent my first eighteen years in a family cult, ruled by my dictatorial father and under the influence of a radically evangelical, end-of-days religion—a double whammy, to be sure.

Despite this upbringing, I'd held dreams of going to college for as long as I could remember—an expectation instilled in me by my mother, who deeply valued education, unlike my father. My parents weren't always religious extremists, you see. They'd both been raised in traditional southern families, attending a middle-of-the-road, southern Baptist church and abiding by the traditional work and family lifestyle of the area in which they were raised.

My father was a dedicated workaholic, self-employed, and consumed by the operations of his welding, charter fishing or commercial fishing businesses, in sequential order. It wasn't until my ninth year that my father underwent his radical religious experience which shifted his focus to becoming a self-employed evangelist instead. He decided that God was calling him to take his previous skills and interests and instead become a "fisherman of men's souls." From that point forward, our lives became increasingly "fringe" as we moved onto a commercial fishing boat, began homeschooling and retreated from mainstream society. The years that followed were tumultuous, confusing and wrought with religious abuse.

Much occurred in the nine years between my father's conversion and the end of my high school career, including multiple moves and eventually re-enrolling in a public high school in southern Georgia. During this time, my father's attention turned from boat ministry to street and motorcycle ministries. I was by his side for each of these turns and compelled by my father to accost strangers in the street to preach "the Good News" through both one on one engagement as well as through the less subtle means of a bullhorn.

Then, in an unexpected twist of fate in the week leading up to my high school graduation, my parents announced their intention to separate. In that moment, the rug was officially pulled out from under the rigid precepts of my entire upbringing. Divorce was a non-option in the religious groups within which I had been deeply indoctrinated. It was unfathomable to me that, after years of my being forced to preach the gospel on street corners as a child, in the midst of all manner of debauchery, from Mardi Gras in New Orleans to Fantasy Fest in Key West, my parents were suddenly calling it quits and calling into question every single grueling, demanding, punitive and rigid religious principle with which I had been beaten down over the previous decade.

It was both a liberation and a complete mind warp. I'd struggled with depression since I was thirteen years old. By the age of seventeen, I'd all but given up on ever meeting the demands of the angry, punitive and yet somehow still "loving" God I'd been taught to fear and obey, just as I feared and obeyed my earthly father. I was a bundle of insecurity, anxiety, doubt, confusion and dread. My parents' sudden announcement turned everything I knew upside down and magnified this bundle of darkness by a hundred percent. Eight weeks later, I went off to college.

After leaving for college at eighteen, I struggled to cope with everyday life under the umbrella of a higher educational institution. Even before learning about my parents' separation, I'd viewed college as my way out—out from under my father's oppressive authority and the constraints of the closed, religious community to which I had been confined for the better part of my short life. I worked hard throughout high school, making straight As to set myself up for the best possible chances of going to a college out of state. My hard work paid off, and with the aid of a generous uncle on my mother's side of the family, I was admitted to a secular, ivy-league college two states away. What I had not anticipated was the total annihilation of all I had ever known, due to the destruction of the family and societal foundation on which I had been raised. Once I "flew the nest," there was no nest to return to, even if I wanted.

College brought all the usual freedom, challenges and exploration it is so well-known for. While going off to college was a step out into the "real world" for many of my peers, I found it to be a well-cushioned fabrication of a "real world", which confounded me. After spending so many days and nights out in the trenches of the *actual* real world, seeing and experiencing first-hand the underbelly of society among the homeless, disabled and drug-addicted cast offs living under bridges, in homeless shelters and in temporary handmade dwellings, college life felt nothing like the real world to me. My peers knew nothing of my background or the kinds of life I'd seen and lived. I felt like a stranger among strangers, a weirdo, and an outcast myself in this newfound "real world."

I was gripped by inner turmoil, reeling from a great deal of unprocessed childhood trauma but with no language or context with which to understand, describe or explain it. There was little common understanding, much less conversation about childhood trauma at that time. I felt like I was just crazy and broken. "There is definitely something wrong with me," I thought. The trauma-induced nightmares and panic attacks started in my sophomore year at the university and would spontaneously occur for the next ten years.

I was urged by my mother and my sister to speak with a psychologist about my deep depressive tendencies. Upon the dissolution of her marriage, my mother immediately began to recede from the extremist religious environment and returned to the middle-of-the-road religious beliefs and societal values of her own upbringing. These values included not only the halls of higher education but the medical and mental health fields, as well. With the distance and separation from my father that college provided, I was free to make some of my own decisions and figure out my own beliefs. I just had no idea yet what they were. However, I knew I was miserable and my mother and sister insisted that a therapist could help. They were worried for my safety.

After a few sessions with one of the school's psychologists, and upon relaying the details of my childhood, I was diagnosed with post-traumatic stress disorder (PTSD), manic depressive disorder and an anxiety disorder with a touch of obsessive compulsive disorder mixed in, just for fun. I was offered an evolving cocktail of psycho-pharmaceuticals over the years that followed. It seemed impossibly simple at that stage. Got issues? Chronically sad and manically emotional? Just take this pill and it will all work itself out!

Unfortunately, despite that early hope in 2000, the medications did not solve my problems as promised and the therapists did not seem to have much else to offer me. Over the next eight years, I was regarded with a mixture of intrigue and shock whenever I spoke to a new therapist or psychiatrist about my childhood, but I found little to no understanding or guidance. Each visit to a new psychologist yielded the same array of diagnoses. At that point, there was little mainstream understanding of post-traumatic stress disorder, much less *complex* post-traumatic stress disorder (C-PTSD) which is only now becoming more commonly known, studied, understood and accepted as a clinical condition. (While C-PTSD is not yet officially recognized in the *Diagnostic and Statistical Manual of Mental Disorders, 5th Edition [DSM V]* used in the United States, it is newly recognized in the *International Classification of Diseases 11th Edition [ICD-11]* which is used by several other countries.)

So without fully understanding why, I barely made it out of the university in one mental and emotional piece. I fought my way through those four years of intense academic pressure, and once I graduated, I was no better off. I earned a Bachelor of Arts in Theater Studies with a minor in Sociology and I had no idea what to do next. I finally had the freedom to pursue my passion for acting, but no skills, confidence or tools for navigating life out on my own.

Back out in the actual real world, after four years under the ivy-covered dome, I found myself utterly floundering in my attempts to accomplish routine, early adulthood tasks, such as finding (and keeping) a job, paying bills and establishing myself as a member of mainstream society. I moved to Charleston, South Carolina, because it was close to my familiar roots, but also promised to offer a thriving theater scene with opportunities to build my acting experience and resume. It also offered some family connections that were mostly cut off by my father during my adolescence, and I hoped to find some safety and comfort in the those familial connections.

I started off working as a waitress during the day and then moved to coffee houses, which allowed me to work mornings and days while I pursued acting and attended rehearsals at night. While I managed to get by with the bare minimum to keep my head above water, I was overwhelmed, miserable, terrified, and feeling stuck every moment of the way. The reconnection with family members did not pan out the way I hoped, as I felt more alien and awkward than ever in their world, due to the gulf created by my early life experiences and its effect on my developmental abilities. Between the years of 2000 and 2016, I worked more than twenty different jobs, ranging from customer service to retail to tourism to administration to tutoring, and I moved more than a dozen times.

I could not understand why I seemed to be so abnormal, so *paralyzed* in my life, and yet so unstable, especially compared to my university peers, who had gone off to grad school or to work in actual professions. In high school, I'd been a high achiever and my classmates joked that I was most likely to become the United States' first female president. I was a driven, educated, highly intelligent young woman with big dreams, but zero capacity to take actual steps toward any concrete structure, goals or plans. At the same time, I had no one to turn to for help or guidance. There was no presence in my day-to-day life to witness the struggle, to see that it was beyond the average early adulthood challenges, or to offer any assistance in navigating this path.

I now know that I was stuck in "freeze mode," where my fight or flight response had so often defaulted to as a child. I still did not understand the degree to which I was reeling from the effects of childhood trauma which marked every year of my life up to that point. Unbeknownst to me, I had little hope of living up to the expectations I held for myself, much less those that I felt others held for me, with no tools or knowledge of what I was up against.

Only now, more than twenty years later, do I finally have the answers and the context for what I was experiencing. Unfortunately, I only came to this awareness after two more decades of mental and emotional torture. Thanks to my early conditioning, and the tattered state of my life as a result, I continued to seek help to fix what I believed to be my utterly flawed and broken essence, and that is how I ended up in the office of a so-called life coach, who fraudulently claimed to be a licensed therapist, and that is why I gradually gave complete control of my life over to this man, who initially offered practical answers and deeper insights into my daily struggle.

In the spring of 2008, I stepped into the office of No Boundaries Life Coaching, Hypnosis & NLP (fictitious name) for the first time, enthusiastically referred by a previous theater buddy with whom I had recently reconnected. I decided to quit taking all my psycho-pharmaceutical meds, for the second time, and had gone off them cold turkey just a handful of months before. Between my frustration with the meds, the side-effects of quitting them, and my ongoing disillusionment with life with or without the meds, I determined that I was going to find a *natural* way to become happy and healthy…or die trying.

The new life coach claimed to have a PhD, to be a Master Practitioner of NLP (Neuro Linguistic Programming) and to have studied many forms of psychology and spirituality. Framed certificates and degrees hung on the wall by his desk. I never looked at them very closely. His business card showed "PhD" after his name. It never occurred to me to question his credentials. It never remotely entered my mind that someone would fabricate all of that and manage to establish a brick-and-mortar business with a steady clientele. His business grew mostly by word of mouth. I, too, was referred to him by a friend who sang his praises which also established a small amount of instant credibility.

The life coach's charisma was undeniable. He was unlike any therapist I had seen before. He was intrigued by my story, but undaunted by it. He was lively and demonstrative, jumping out of his seat, raising his voice and gesturing broadly to make his point at times and then pulling back, speaking in a calm and measured tone at other times. He seemed to have an answer for everything.

After a couple of sessions of learning my history and about every person in my life as part of his "intake" process, the dynamic shifted to where he did far more of the talking than I did. I saw him for a two-hour session every single week for the first year. I found the fact that he offered two hour sessions, rather than the standard fifty-five minutes which rarely provided sufficient time to delve into the issues I hoped to address, surprising and refreshing. In the beginning, these sessions were extremely affordable compared to my previous therapists. A two hour session was only eighty dollars. That was still a lot of money for me to be dishing out on a weekly basis, working as a barista and living paycheck to paycheck, but my need for help was high and I was strongly encouraged by him to continue investing in my personal and spiritual growth with these sessions. I was told that if I trusted, and if I truly valued the work we were doing, the funds would be provided. I scraped by, prioritizing these sessions financially. Many of the spiritual and self-help books that he initially introduced also served to convince me that it was up to me to manifest the abundance that I required to afford these sessions.

Within a couple of months, the life coach was established as not only my therapist but my spiritual teacher, and I, his eager student. I was given homework assignments which included not only those books to read, but also worksheets to do. Having worked hard as a student for so much of my life, this role resonated and appealed to me. After all, I was certain I had no idea what I was doing in life.

The materials, teachers and authors he introduced me to opened up a whole new world and a whole new way of seeing it. While this life coach was not the author of any of these ideas or techniques, he subtly got credit for all of them as the teacher who introduced me to them and "taught" them to me. The concepts introduced in these materials breathed fresh air into my life. They introduced me to a spirituality that made far more sense than that of my childhood. They empowered me to make real changes in my life, starting with my mindset. They taught me that I was the author of my reality and therefore responsible for my experience of life. They showed me how to proactively shift that experience through technique and repetition.

Many of these lessons were truly helpful and I have carried the fundamental truth of them with me into my new life, post-cult. Every high control group offers some value at the outset which serves to draw us into that world in the first place. Without it, we would skip on by. These profound lessons and truths were the bit of goodness that drew me into the cultic quagmire and they are the bit of goodness I endeavor to retain and effectively utilize now that I am free.

During this early revelatory period, the life coach established an incredible rapport with me. He openly shared all manner of details about his life, from his years of pursuing a music career to details about his former relationships to his (supposed) mystical experiences and deep learning under the guidance of his own guru, a yogi from the Far East. He gave great big bear hugs at the end of our sessions, further breaking the stereotype of the traditional therapist. It was in part this break from the mold that promised to provide me with some real answers and genuine life-changing help that did not require medications. After all, no other therapist had provided such resources, such insight or such a personal connection. No other therapist had been so lively, so demonstrative and so full of conviction about the issues they spoke of. No other therapist talked this much. No other therapist was so direct and strong in their recommendations and suggestions about what I should or should not do. No other therapist had been so commanding, so radical in his approach or so authoritative. While I could not see it at the time, because their personalities and externals seemed so different, no other therapist had been so much like *my father*.

As time went on, the stories of the life he had lived and the places he had been grew bigger and bigger. After establishing that initial trust as a safe, welcoming and helpful space for me to be myself and rapidly receive answers to my burning questions about life and the universe, I was less and less likely to question his intentions or sincerity. The tales he shared about his grand adventures and humble spiritual achievements served to create a larger-than-life presence imbued with deep wisdom. I felt that the Universe had finally sent me my own mentor and guide, that the tides had finally turned in my favor, that the sun might finally shine in my life. For the first time, I had hope.

Many of the teachings, authors and resources he introduced were profoundly helpful and healing…in a way. The tools and techniques that they taught could be used to completely shift the trajectory of my life, from the inside out, for the better. Unfortunately, just as has been done with other spiritual texts and teachings for centuries, these tools can also be twisted and weaponized. In the wrong hands where they are subjected to another man's interpretations and agendas, these teachings can be effectively used to control, manipulate, oppress and destroy. The desire for power, control and fame historically leads to corruption. For a man who had spent the first half of his life striving, and ultimately failing, to achieve status as a rock star, the allure of setting up his own tiny kingdom as a spiritual guru of sorts—to be highly regarded and devoutly followed by his self-made microscopic community of dedicated clients—was very great. He succumbed to the temptation and a dozen of his longest standing clients paid the price. I was one of them.

After fourteen years under this man's constant influence and progressively coercive control, which culminated in the final three years under his complete and total control, I broke free for the first time in my life. I finally began to learn about trauma, complex PTSD, cultic abuse, malignant narcissism and every resulting symptom experienced by survivors of these influences. At that point, I began to understand why my life had always been such a struggle, why I made the choices I did, and how I ended up in that situation. I'd lost just about everything I ever had...but I wasn't dead yet. There was only one thing left for me to do, as far as I could see. I must start over from scratch and rebuild a life worth living. I decided to claw my way out of the dark depths in which I was buried for so long, *determined* to find a future full of light. My success in this endeavor is an act of defiance. It is my personal rebellion against the systems of control that have been used to manipulate and *almost* destroy me.

At the time of this writing, it has been a mere three years since I emerged back into the light of day, escaping cultic control and stepping back into the "real world" once more. It has been a long, painful, arduous journey. It has come with some great highs and some awful lows. This time around, however, the information and resources for folks like me, both cult survivors and every other kind of C-PTSD survivor, is burgeoning into mainstream consciousness.

I managed to get out of the high-control group right at the point in time when a plethora of support and awareness was finally flowing freely toward this very issue and #igotout was quietly following the #metoo movement[1]. That is how I learned that I was not alone, and that is how I began to finally gain some tools for coping with my experiences while also navigating everyday life—an overwhelming feat for those of us

[1] Similar to the #metoo hashtag which went viral in 2017, a social movement used to raise awareness and give a voice to survivors of sexual assault, harassment and exploitation, the #igotout movement started in 2020 to give a voice to survivors of high control, coercive and cultic abuse.

emerging from long-term trauma and attempting to establish a healthy, balanced, "normal" life—something some of us may have never known.

Upon escaping these cultic clutches, I dedicated myself to my own healing and recovery over the days and months that followed. It seemed like the only option for me if I ever wanted to achieve the type of life I'd always dreamed of: a life of stability, a life of fulfillment and a life of personal passion. As in my twenties, I sought to learn how to "fix" myself so I could finally get on with experiencing the life of goodness and fulfillment which I had always dreamed of.

I dove in and out of phases of healing and recovery. Eventually, I began to understand that every step I took was a part of the process of getting myself, and my life, back—even the periods where it felt like I was doing nothing at all. I became curious about my own process. I suddenly began to suspect the answers to my own recovery could be found in studying my personal process of recovery, a process that was informed and built by all the amazing resources now available to me, coupled with the innate wisdom I had gained from my many years of suffering in personal darkness, dedicated to self-help and personal development studies. During those fourteen years under increasing cultic control, I devoted myself entirely to intense introspection, deconstruction and self-awareness. The process of self-analysis had become second nature, but now I faced the task of transforming those practices from tools of self-condemnation and destruction into tools of gentle, kind and loving self-support.

It was in this decision—to find my own answers within myself, based on my intuition and the lessons I had already learned during my recovery period—that brought me to my notebook to begin penning *The Journey Back to Self*. It occurred to me then that my desire and my intention was not only to help *myself,* but to put together a practical, simple and approachable guide that I could have benefited from at the time I became free. I wanted to create a booklet with which I could go back in time some three years and place in my own hands, synthesized and distilled, the tools I had collected to expedite my process of healing. It is my hope and my desire that it should do the same for you, my friend.

Having said that, I firmly believe that every single soul's journey is unique to them and there is absolutely NO one-size-fits-all approach to healing and recovery, *from* anything or *for* anyone. I offer this book to you as one more simple guide with a handful of practical tools to add to your personal journey. If any single part of this manuscript helps even one person, then its purpose has been fulfilled. I invite you to use what appeals to you, to practice what resonates with you and to toss out every last thing that does not work, apply or add benefit for you.

Your journey is your own. It is unlike anyone else's. You will travel along it *at your own pace.* Even during the times you feel like you are doing nothing at all, you may be doing *exactly* what is needed. I urge you not to compare or judge yourself. There is simply no comparison possible in this journey, because there are no two journeys exactly alike. In the same way, I have learned that there is truly no final destination. The purpose of the journey is continued growth, healing and ever-increasing levels of happiness. It has no end. We will never "arrive." For survivors and all those coping with CPTSD, we will do this recovery work to varying degrees for the rest of our lives, so there is truly no way to measure the process. All you have to do is be in it and keep moving forward. Be gentle, patient and compassionate with yourself. If you do nothing else, that alone will suffice.

1

Before the Clouds Part

Getting Started

Sooo...*now what??*

You made it out. You made it through. You're on the other side of "it." Whatever your "it" may be. You're a *survivor*.

I hate to be the one to say it, but if you're reading this book, I suspect you already know: the work is just beginning. The period of trauma, or traumatic event, may be in your rear view mirror, but what most of us find is that there is now a daunting mountain rising before us and there is no easy way around it. Now, the climb up—*the recovery*—begins.

To an outside observer, it may seem that your star is on the rise. After all, you're free and you're alive! The world is your oyster! Good for you for overcoming those trials and tribulations. Go ahead and give yourself a big ol' pat on the back. You did it! The storm clouds are all behind you now—it's time to turn that frown upside down. Sunshine and rainbows await!

I encountered this mentality at times when I first broke free. It triggered a sense of shame and guilt because that was not how I felt at all. Unfortunately, that is not how trauma, or trauma recovery, works. At first, things may seem to get even worse before they get better. If that's the case for you, it does not inherently mean that you are doing anything wrong. It is just part of the process. Like after any natural disaster, there is an overwhelming amount of clean-up work to do. Everyday life has been turned on its head. There is disorientation, upheaval and still an enormous amount of pain that has nowhere to go (or so it may seem). The task of setting things right takes time, work and conscious effort. It is a process, and in some sense, that process will continue for the rest of our lives.

When I was eleven years old, I got to experience the effects of a Category Four hurricane first hand; it was Hurricane Andrew which decimated parts of southern Florida. It wasn't my first hurricane, but it was my first time living in the aftermath of a hurricane, one of the most devastating on record at that point in time.

I remember the initial hours and subsequent days after the storm passed. We loaded up in my father's truck and ventured north from the Florida Keys on US Hwy 1, through the Everglades, onto the mainland. We were unable to progress very far due to the wreckage. I can recall seeing parts of houses missing, a piece of steel from a road sign run straight through the trunk of a palm tree, creating handlebars on either side. The surreality was overwhelming. It was mind-bending to look up into a tree and see common household items—a spatula, a chair, a curling iron—suspended in the branches. Folks stood outside their former homes, in the street, staring listlessly, disoriented, unable to compute the world that surrounded them, completely unrecognizable from the world they knew a mere forty-eight hours before. Time stood still.

After that pause of shock, in true human nature, the work of survival and rebuilding ensued. Chainsaws buzzed, generators droned, hammers pounded and the clean-up of the world was suddenly in motion. It was hard, grueling, sweaty work and it went on for months, years. In many ways, those areas would never be the same again.

It is much the same for trauma survivors.

That is not to say, however, that it does not get easier. I truly believe it does. But "easier" isn't really the right word. It gets more familiar, more comfortable and more doable, over time. Once you find the right gear to help you navigate your path, that is.

Before I found my groove, things actually got worse in many ways. Like undergoing a surgery, the recovery process may initially feel as painful *or more* painful than the condition for which the surgery was required. Recovering from trauma requires the same level of work, sweat and difficulty as the gargantuan task of rebuilding after any disaster. From busting through trauma bonds to navigating the colorful array of C-PTSD symptoms that sprout like weeds throughout your life, sometimes quite unexpectedly—let's just call it what it is: Recovery is a bitch.

There is no one way over, or through, that mountain of recovery. Each of us must find our own path. But thank God, there *are* resources and those resources are multiplying by the day. Never has there been a better time, I think, to recover from trauma than right now, when trauma-informed consciousness is on the steady rise. My hope is that this book can be one of those resources for you and provide you with some practical ideas and tools to incorporate along your trek.

Spoiler alert: There is no "fix" for us. Although I sought to "fix" myself since my early twenties, only in my recent recovery journey have I truly begun to understand the very legitimate reasons that we cannot be "fixed". One practical reason: Healing and growth is a lifelong process. There is no endpoint or final destination to reach. So long as we are breathing, we are evolving at whatever pace we choose. Secondly—and this is an important one—*we cannot fix ourselves* because, at our core, *we are not broken.* Trauma survivors are resilient and resourceful creatures and we have accumulated myriad ways of coping and navigating our circumstances. Those mechanisms of survival have served a vital purpose, and now that we have survived, we face the task of learning a new way of functioning, relating and navigating within the world. It is a pivot. It is a reformatting. There is nothing inherently wrong *with* us. There is something terribly wrong about what happened *to* us. *You are not broken.*

Ultimately, this journey of recovery is a process of learning to reconnect with our true self, the one we completely lost among the traumas. Over these first three years of recovery, I have steadily climbed that mountain of processing-and-healing from a lifetime of coercive control, abusive authority and the effects of long-term, ongoing trauma. What I have discovered is that the key to long-term recovery, and the foundation upon which all true healing lies, is developing a loving relationship with yourself. The fractured and fragmented parts of us must be put back together into one integrated, unified and cohesive whole. This requires simultaneous healing on every level of our being: mental, emotional, physical and spiritual.

But what does that look like? And how is it done? These are the questions we will address here in a simple, layman's guide, not only to the early stages of recovery, but to learning to love yourself like you've never been loved before. The chapters that follow are full of suggestions and ideas for you to try out. Not all of them will work for you and not all of them will you even want to try. My goal is not to tell anyone else how to heal; rather, it is to offer a distilled version of my own process, one that may help you to expedite your own journey; or, if nothing else, perhaps to make the process a little more pleasant and a little less lonesome.

As I explained earlier, I set out to put this book together with myself in mind. I wanted to create a resource that, if placed into my own hands within the first weeks or months after I got out of the high-control group, would have offered me clear-cut action steps that I could consciously take to initiate my recovery process, all laid out in a simple, approachable, easy-to-digest format. In order to do this, I have taken the steps that worked best for me so far on this journey, through trial and error, and distilled them into sections that loosely build on one another toward a trajectory of overall health and well-being. Spending a bit of time on each step, in the order presented, may best prepare you to integrate the next step presented. Having said that, I recognize that your journey will be different from mine and unique from all others. As a result, I encourage you to try out whatever areas most appeal to you at any given moment.

Despite my initial inspiration, the motivating factor that propelled me to complete this piece of work was having *you* in mind. This book is intended for anyone who has chosen to heal, regardless of where you are in your personal healing and development process. Whether you are days or decades out of a traumatic or abusive experience, the importance of mending the broken connections between our Mind,

Body and Spirit remains fundamental to our healing. I have found that for this reintegration process to be effective and long-term, it must be centered and rooted in love for ourselves, first and foremost.

The journey of healing and growth is not a linear one; rather, it tends to follow one of the fundamental patterns of nature. As we proceed, we wind our way through layers of darkness, fear and muck. We travel up that mountain, encountering switchbacks, steep ascents, sudden declines, and gradually progressing toward higher and higher summits. Just as we find that beautiful spiral known as the Fibonacci sequence represented throughout countless aspects of nature from a snail shell to the structure of DNA to the Milky Way itself, so do we find this pattern metaphorically in the healing journey. This means that we will encounter the seemingly same issues, come up against similar obstacles, and battle the same-looking demons repeatedly throughout our process. It can be tempting to become discouraged when we re-encounter a personal issue or block that we thought we already overcame some time before. We may decide that we have not made any progress at all. Not so, my friend, not so. We are circling a mountain. We start from where we are and we begin to walk that path, so that each time we encounter the "same issue" we are actually arriving at it on a new level, at a new depth. And so it goes, as we steadily progress, around and around, higher and higher, with increasing pockets of light and happiness extending into broader and broader expanses of our lives.

Finally, I would like to make it abundantly clear that I am not a mental health professional and I do not believe that there is any one right or wrong way to traverse this path. I certainly do not claim to have all the answers. I am writing to you from a personal perspective, from one survivor to another who is actively navigating these tumultuous waters. I am presenting the core truths I have discovered about my own healing journey and the techniques that have proven most essential in navigating it. Regardless of where you already are in the spiral of healing, I hope that you will find new ideas and inspirations for reintegrating your whole self from a place of gentleness and love.

In my experience, the hardest part of any new project is always *getting started.* However, we are resilient creatures. We are survivors, overcomers, rebuilders. Complex trauma survivors are often among the most emotionally intelligent, compassionate, self-aware, deep and unfathomably strong humans I have ever encountered. You may not understand how you made it through, you may even wish sometimes that you hadn't, that you didn't have to face the next day, but you are here, and you will persevere. If you've made it to this point, you have a warrior's spirit within you yet. It *can* get better, and if you determine for yourself that you will see that light once again, it *will* get better. Mount up, warrior. You have so much goodness yet to offer *and* to experience. Set your mind on your desired outcome and commit yourself to the journey: It's time to get started.

2

Step One: Stop, Drop & Listen

"Trauma" is a word that gets tossed about quite commonly these days. I find it is often used to refer to any unfortunate or negative experience someone has encountered. Hard times, grief, loss, bad experiences and periods of darkness are a part of every human being's life, but that doesn't necessarily make them traumatic. Google "what is trauma" and you will find, "Trauma is defined as a deeply distressing or disturbing event that **overwhelms a person's ability to cope,** causing significant and lasting negative consequences" (Google AI Overview; added emphasis). Canada's Centre for Addiction and Mental Health (CAMH) website states, "We all respond to injury in different ways. Trauma is the emotional response when an injury overwhelms us" (https://www.camh.ca/en/health-info/guides-and-publications/trauma).

When a fearful and negative experience overwhelms our body and mind's capacity to process it, trauma is the result. Since every person will react to, and process, a situation in their own way, two people can undergo the exact same experience but perceive it differently, and therefore walk away with different impacts. How fascinating is that?

It is not defined so much by *what* traumatic event happened to you, where, why, when or how. If the event or situation overwhelms your internal systems to the point of inducing a state of fight, flight, freeze or fawn[2]—depending upon the degree and severity of that event—trauma can result. In the case of an isolated incident of severe trauma, a person may suffer from post-traumatic stress disorder (PTSD), a condition in which the body and mind continue to suffer from distressing physical and psychological symptoms caused by the event long after the occurrence.

In the case of individuals who lived under circumstances of ongoing and repeated traumatic events, such as living in a war zone, trapped by cultic control, growing up with abusive parents, or living with an abusive partner (just to name a few), then you may have developed complex post-traumatic stress disorder (C-PTSD) and may be experiencing its effects in your day-to-day life. Regardless of the specific circumstances of the trauma you endured, you spent a prolonged period of time living in survival mode, with all the accompanying impacts on your brain, your body, your mind and your emotions. Living a life of coping and surviving on a day-to-day, even minute-to-minute basis disrupts our natural equilibrium physically, mentally, emotionally and spiritually.

---

[2] The human fight or flight mechanism is a physiological acute stress response to perceived danger in which chemicals and hormones are released within the body to prepare it to either face (fight) or escape (flee) the threat. There are two more stress responses that are somewhat lesser known and round out the "Four Fs" of fear response in animals: freeze and fawn. The freeze response is one in which the victim shuts down entirely becoming immobile and unresponsive, such as playing dead to avoid detection. The fawn response is one in which the victim attempts to appease or placate the threat in order to avoid attack and harm.

The impacts can be devastating to our health on every one of these levels.

When the mechanisms of survival are screaming in your ears all the damn time, it becomes difficult, if not impossible, to hear anything else. Once we manage to escape the traumatic situation, it can take quite a while for us to calm down, think clearly, feel clearly (or feel at all), relax, and hear our own unique, true voice speaking within us once again. We have been running ragged for so long, struggling against every obstacle to maintain some sense of stability in a chaotic, unpredictable, fearful, and oftentimes threatening place. When all that stops, it can be disorienting, at best, and downright terrifying, at worst. In some cases, it may not all stop at once. Although the external circumstances may have changed, it takes time for our bodies, minds and hearts to catch up to this new reality. The time it takes will be different for each person, and the process we undergo during that time will be unique as well; however, we can help each other to navigate the new challenge of learning to live life in trauma recovery.

By my final three years in the therapy cult, I had no remaining autonomy and very little privacy. I worked incessantly. My leader was also my employer and I had to be at his beck and call at all hours of the day and night. He might suddenly want a work task completed at 12 am, just as I was about to fall asleep, and if I did not jump up to comply, I could be assured of emotional and mental duress from the yelling, berating or shunning that would ensue. On top of this unpredictable and volatile state, I was subjected to constant noise. Even as I slept, a TV played throughout the night, flashing perpetual technicolor lights and streaming the music, dialogue and sound effects of an old, popular TV show. During waking hours, again, always, some noise either from electronics or the endless talking from the leader. Nowhere and at no time was there peace and quiet in my environment, all of which continually rubbed my nerves raw. On the rare occasion I might get to spend some time out in nature, on a hiking trail for example, the leader would drone on and on in a diatribe, or engage us in impossible questions and speculations, never allowing a moment for stillness or quiet.

Upon my release from this prison of constant noise and motion, I craved stillness and quiet, but it took time to literally detox the noise from my mind, body and life. For months after I escaped, my ears rang from the relative quiet of the world around me. It was very uncomfortable and unsettling. I wondered if it would ever stop. I would later learn that ringing in the ears is one of many symptoms of trauma with which I would have to patiently grapple. In addition, the thoughts in my mind seemed to be shouting at me. Again, it would take time to understand that my thoughts *had* to shout to have any chance of being heard over all the incessant noise. Only once they began to be consistently heard and acknowledged did they begin to gradually reduce in volume.

Step one in this practical guide is to learn to be still, be quiet and *listen*. "Listen to what?" you might ask. The birds, the wind, the traffic, the sound of silence, but most of all, to *ourselves*.

Sometimes, when we are incapable of accomplishing this task, our bodies will suddenly force us into stillness through some sort of malady. Illnesses are common in the initial stages of trauma recovery, as our internal systems finally begin to detox the excess hormones from survival mode and attempt to find health and equilibrium. It can be incredibly jarring to come to a halt after living under the systems that created complex post-traumatic stress disorder. Nevertheless, being still is one of the most accessible and most badly needed gifts that we can offer to ourselves when we take our first steps toward recovery.

In my first year outside of the cult, I required what seemed to me to be an excessive amount of lying around, sleeping, and long periods of non-activity. This need felt like a limitation and I found it incredibly frustrating. I finally had my freedom, after all. I wanted to go out and enjoy it! See the world! Explore! Go places, meet people, *do* things! But alas, I absolutely could not. Neither my brain nor my body would permit it except in the tiniest, briefest of spurts. Every part of my being was exhausted and I did not have the mental or emotional bandwidth for much social interaction at all.

Four months into my newfound freedom and recovery, I found myself in a new job, in a new city, surrounded by new people in a new office environment with a communal workspace. By the end of each workday, any little bit of energetic reserves I had were long gone. For the first six months, I mostly came home and plopped in my armchair in front of the TV in my tiny basement apartment, where I re-watched *Gilmore Girls* in its entirety, punctuated by lighthearted movies that required little mental digestion. This was all I could do and it was absolutely what I needed. I needed time and space to just be physically still.

There were the occasional weekends where I barely got out of bed, much less left my apartment. I required that entire time to recuperate from the week behind and rejuvenate for the week ahead. And I also got sick—quite a bit. In my first eighteen months out of the cult, I fell prey to seven different physical maladies, from colds and flus to a stomach ulcer. My immune system, just like the rest of my body's systems, was completely depleted, so I was extremely susceptible to illness which then further required rest and stillness.

Once I finally accepted my current limitations and extended grace to myself in light of those, I began to allow myself to enjoy and appreciate this stillness, which I had not known in so very long. It gave me a chance to quietly think and slowly process, bit by tiny bit. As the raging force of survival mode slowly, gradually subsided, and I allowed myself to be still, I began to hear my own natural, internal voice rising back up to the surface ever so meekly.

Suspending Judgment

I learned that indulging this voice, and the little whims and wants of my internal world, were the way to go. Even if those whims or wants weren't always the healthiest of desires, I needed to break free from the life of restriction, deprivation and control under which I had come to live for so long. I decided to indulge the inner voice, which was sometimes just my inner child, when it would speak up. I learned to strike bargains to balance those desires with healthy counterparts. When my inner child wanted to retreat from the work of self-care and just go crazy feasting on Little Debbie snack cakes and pop tarts because "nothing really matters anyway" and "making real food is too much work," I would give myself a day and indulge her. Then, hop back in the saddle the next morning and begin again.

It was so important, so necessary and so healing for me to *suspend judgment* of myself and to allow myself to just be wherever I was in the moment, physically, mentally and emotionally. When we emerge from these controlling and abusive environments, there are, without question, a litany of rules and regulations that we have absorbed and learned to embody. Sometimes these ways of being, seeing and operating within the world have become so ingrained, so second nature, that we do not even realize that they are inorganic to us. Most often, we have learned to police ourselves to operate within the limitations and restrictions of those oppressive environments in order to stay safe. Breaking the rules—whether they be spoken or unspoken—comes with a set of consequences which may involve a wide range of abuses, but always includes harsh judgment.

Cultic and high-control groups (or relationships) involve an "us versus them" dynamic. This dynamic includes judgment of others, and to stay safely within the boundaries of the "us," one must abide by the parameters of that group's system. Learning to suspend judgment of ourselves, therefore, becomes a crucial act in the process of internal liberation. It is one thing to physically escape the confines of these abusive systems, but it is another thing entirely to escape the psychological, emotional and spiritual confines they created within us. The journey of recovery, therefore, can be said to be the internal exodus from these oppressive systems. Suspending judgment of yourself and allowing yourself to move in a way that is authentic, natural and healing *for you* is a powerful act of rebellion against your abusive past.

For me, allowing myself to do nothing, to sleep in, to eat whatever I wanted, to be "unproductive" and "lazy" (internal judgments) through long periods of rest was a luxury, but it was a terrifying one because of those harsh internalized judgments formed over a lifetime of oppressive and abusive environments wherein these behaviors were not permitted. For the most part, I offered myself these luxuries in the solitude of my own home, since no one in my new world was aware of my situation, nor was I comfortable with sharing any of it. So, at the end of the workday, I learned to allow myself to be tired, "lazy," feel like a wreck, be unproductive, indulge in "childish" wants, and generally, go easy on myself. This did not come naturally at first. Ironically, it took a lot of work to stop working so hard. I didn't see it that way at the time, but in reality, letting go of the many ways in which I was programmed to think and behave through coercive control, and releasing the judgments of myself that I accumulated along the way, was a tremendous amount of work.

Being still, which was such an unfamiliar luxury, was one of the hardest things I had to do. At the same time, I didn't have much choice, since my body repeatedly told me of its current limitations in the language of crushing fatigue and recurring illness. I decided to listen to my body and to the little voice in my mind that kept advocating for gentleness. I found that being kind and loving to myself was so much easier than the alternative of condemnation and judgment that had been forced on me over the previous decades. In fact, I found that I was really great at being loving toward myself without those constant external influences (the endless voice of the group's leader) pushing me toward punitive mindsets and behaviors. I began to devote myself to, well, *myself*, and that informed the entire process of recovery I had embarked on.

The single most important first step that I discovered on my own path of recovery was learning to identify *my* internal voice—distinct from the voices of the punitive authority figures and abusers who previously ruled in my mind—and to listen to *myself*. It is essential on my journey, because that basic human right was denied me for such a long time. It is important to note that this learning-to-listen-to-myself business is an ongoing, long-term project.

I especially determined that I would listen *only* to myself when it came to navigating this path of recovery, and I encourage you to do the same. That is not to say that I refused to seek help, guidance or education about this process. On the contrary, I delved into learning about my situation and discovering just how many of us have endured similar misfortunes. This education reinforced my desire to commit myself to my own recovery. I absorbed these resources as informational tools, but I constantly checked myself from deferring to them as authoritative sources of ultimate truth, as I had done with other voices in the past. Rather, I took what made sense to me, what worked for me, and held onto that alone.

Learning to Be Still

Learning to listen and being still often go hand in hand. Allowing ourselves periods of non-activity just to *be* invites us to sit at the table with ourselves and hear what we have to say. This takes practice and repetition, but as we create pockets of time and space to be still with ourselves and listen as we live our daily life, we can uncover deeper layers of insight and clarity from within our own hearts and minds. These insights will be our ultimate guide along the way of recovery from trauma, but to get them, we have to put in the "work" of doing nothing.

I'd like to clarify at the outset that being still is not the same thing as numbing out or being stuck in freeze mode which is a consequence of the ongoing engagement of the freeze response coping mechanism during trauma-inducing times. For those of us who frequently defaulted to the freeze response during traumatic situations, our body and mind can get stuck in this mode as if out of habit[3]. As a result, any form of stress can trigger this response within our nervous system, and it may effectively shut us down in a way that no longer serves to protect us but rather inhibits our ability to move fluidly and productively through our lives. Simple, everyday tasks, such as making a phone call to schedule an appointment, may feel literally impossible to accomplish for an individual who is stuck in freeze mode (also known as functional freeze). This state of being can cause enormous frustration for those experiencing it and may be incomprehensible to an outside observer, but it is a protective mechanism gone rogue as a result of ongoing trauma.

While being in freeze mode does not qualify as its healthy counterpart of consciously being still, it is crucial that we do *not* beat ourselves up for freeze response behaviors when we are engaged in them. I have struggled with freeze mode since I was a young adult and one thing I have learned is that the guilt and shame I feel around it only make it harder to overcome. Because stress can serve to further mire us in the freeze response, it is so important for us to be gentle, kind and compassionate with ourselves as we're beginning the conscious process of healing and recovery. Regardless of which stress response became your primary, you developed the coping mechanisms that you use for very good reasons, and at one point in time, they served you well. They

---

[3] The Four Fs of fear response in animals (fight, flight, freeze and fawn) are a primal response to perceived danger. While we may utilize any or all of these responses when a threat is presented, most of us will have a primary response or two that we most frequently default to in times of distress. Functional freeze results when the freeze response remains activated long after the genuine threat has passed. If you'd like to dive deeper, visit: https://www.bannerhealth.com/healthcareblog/teach-me/functional-freeze-mode-what-it-is-and-how-to-break-free and https://khironclinics.com/blog/functional-freeze-emotions-after-trauma/.

were designed to help you survive, and if you're sitting here reading this book now, then they worked! We can thank that part of ourselves for helping us to make it through the hardest challenges of our life so far and acknowledge them for their desire and effort to keep us safe. Having done that, we can begin to un-learn and un-train ourselves from defaulting to those mechanisms now that our circumstances have changed and we've chosen to heal.

At the same time as you are learning to be still and to listen, you may also require periods of completely zoning out and shutting off, as I did when I came home each night and marathoned *Gilmore Girls* until it was time for bed. If this is what you need, that is okay too. In order to effectively do the work of healing, we must create a safe space, both *within* and *around* us, from which to do that work. It is not realistic for us to take on enormous amounts of pain, fear and confusion from prolonged trauma and to delve into it headfirst day after day. Rather, we chip away at it as our courage and our strength allows, but we must also be willing to challenge ourselves to deal with the uncomfortable feelings and thoughts whenever we can, pushing ourselves gently to not *always* run from them or *always* avoid them. You must become the master of finding this balance within yourself: the balance of gentle, compassionate caregiver and fearless, determined warrior who will push you forward into the next chapter of your life. You need *both* of them.

Unlike freeze mode, being still and learning to listen are active, conscious behaviors. It is a process of sitting quietly by yourself and allowing yourself to feel whatever sensations are in your body, feel whatever emotions are lying just under the surface, and hear whatever thoughts are running through your mind. Sometimes, these feelings and thoughts will be loud and clear, up front and in your face.

Sometimes, they will be more elusive and require a bit of sussing out. That is why it is necessary to allow time and space to explore them and sit with them. It will also require a great deal of courage and determination, because sitting with the feelings and thoughts can be extremely painful and scary at times. However, avoiding them endlessly will not allow them to transform, will not allow you to learn from them and will not enable them to ever go away.

There are no rules about how much time a sitting-and-listening session takes. It will vary by the situation and the amount of time you can afford. It may take three minutes of stillness for you to tune in and work out what your mind, body and heart are telling you, or it may take an hour. It is a practice that we incorporate into our day-to-day lives, and over time, it becomes easier, more natural and increasingly informative.

You do not have to *do* anything with the thoughts, feelings and sensations that you discover. That can come later. All that is necessary is to hear them, acknowledge them and *suspend judgment* of them as much as you possibly can. If you do feel compelled to take some sort of action, be sure you have first allowed yourself to fully experience what is coming up. It is tempting to use the "doing" to escape the experience. Despite any discomfort these sensations and thoughts may entail, they have hidden gifts for you in the form of information, insights, transformation and release.

Feeling Your Feelings: "You can't heal what you can't feel"

Shutting down our feelings or cutting ourselves off from them is a common coping mechanism during intense or prolonged periods of difficulty. Many of us engage in this practice to the point that we are no longer sure what our feelings are. Oftentimes, it is seen as a sign of strength or resilience. In some cultures, it is encouraged as a quality of toughness or self-control. Unfortunately, while this coping mechanism of disconnection may have been necessary at the time, in a positively functioning life, it is not a sign of strength or resilience or health.

On top of that, one of the defining characteristics of high-control groups and relationships is being taught or told what to think and feel. We are not permitted to feel or express our genuine feelings unless they fall in line with the approved view or agenda of the leader. Finally, gaslighting is a common tool used in high-control situations to further separate us from ourselves by methodically eroding our sense of self and connection to our own thoughts and feelings. While the term is used casually in popular culture today, gaslighting is actually a form of psychological manipulation that is exerted tactically and over time to gradually degrade an individual's sense of reality and cause them to question their own judgment, memories, and interpretation of events. This tool serves to further destabilize the individual and fosters even greater dependence upon the group, leader, or abuser. It causes intense psychological harm and leaves the individual in a fragmented state mentally and emotionally.

For all of these reasons, reconnecting with our true feelings and the thoughts behind them is a fundamental aspect of healing the divide between our hearts, minds and bodies. An enormous amount of power and information lies within the walls of our boarded up feelings. Gently tearing down these internal barriers is a central and ongoing part of our healing journey. Feeling our feelings repairs the internal bridges between the heart, mind, and body, reconnecting us with our true self.

Wisdom tells us, "The only way to get to the other side is to *go through it,*" or as I like to say, "the only way *to* it is *through* it!" We *must* feel our feelings and experience everything that comes with them if we want to heal. There is absolutely NO way around this. Feeling your feelings, especially those devastatingly dark and painful ones, well…that is *true* strength and the sign of some serious, bad ass bravery. The practice of being still and learning to listen reconnects us to our feelings and the thoughts behind them. It is the doorway to healing. We must identify *what* we are feeling, and *what* we are thinking that is informing those feelings, in order to bring light and air to these dark places.

After spending fourteen years in what became a spirituality-based therapy cult, I was no stranger to sitting with feelings. While in the group, I spent a solid two hours every single morning critically addressing my feelings through a practice we called "forgiveness worksheets". However, I *was* a stranger to holding non-judgmental, open space for myself in those feelings. I'd spent so much time being judged and shamed for my feelings, both by myself and others, that the act of allowing the feelings within me to surface as both a physical and emotional experience without critically analyzing them was absolutely foreign.

Once again, we find that the path to internal liberation requires suspending all those judgments that we have absorbed over a lifetime. These judgments may have been internalized from the family mentality in which you were raised, from the traumatic situation you escaped, or from your society at large. It is likely an interwoven combination of these influences, among others. Regardless of the source, a significant amount of our pain stems from these judgments and effectively deters us from bravely and honestly feeling our feelings.

The truth is that our feelings are not good *or* bad, despite our incessant need to categorize them. Feelings just *are*. They are informed by our thoughts, and while our thoughts may arise and recede at random, we do not have to believe every single thought that arises in our minds. Indeed, we get to choose which thoughts we invest in, and in so doing, we may also choose which feelings to nurture and cultivate. However, we cannot deal with what we refuse to acknowledge is there. We must bring conscious awareness to our minds, hearts and bodies to discover what is there so that we may intentionally choose whether we wish to continue investing in the thoughts and feelings that are quietly informing our lives. We must *feel* in order to *deal* and ultimately *heal* our minds, hearts and bodies.

When we extend grace to ourselves and suspend judgment of our feelings, it allows us to tap into greater stores of courage and curiosity in our healing process. Non-judgment and curiosity are like the headlamp and the map to our internal exploration. They shine a light on what lies within us so that our deepest feelings may emerge and guide us to what needs uncovering next. As we gently allow these painful parts of ourselves to surface, a significant amount of healing can be done by simply offering loving kindness and understanding to ourselves.

Listen, I understand how great the fight can be within us to avoid feeling our feelings. Our society encourages us to numb and avoid our feelings on a daily basis. We are spoon-fed a vast array of mechanisms whereby we may easily accomplish this self-sabotage, through drugs and alcohol, food, social media, sex and romantic relationships, compulsive shopping and more. I know how unappealing this invitation to *feel* may be. In fact, it may seem downright dangerous—irresponsible even! If we really allow ourselves to go there, we don't know what will happen, what we'll end up doing or if we'll ever be able to return from that edge. We secretly suspect that it would destroy us, that we would not survive, that there would be no coming back from that abyss.

It is true that the feelings of pain resulting from trauma can be intense. That is why I want to take a moment to not only acknowledge this reality but to stress the importance of feeling our feelings *safely*. It is my hope that the tools and processes offered in this book will assist you in accomplishing this. Because these feelings can be so overwhelming, it is important that we navigate them with patience and kindness toward ourselves. By honing in on the inherent wisdom of our own intuition (which we will discuss in the next chapter), exercising patience with ourselves as we dip into the work of healing and then take breaks as needed, and offering compassion to ourselves through the suspension of self-judgment, we can safely wade through the waters of emotion that are swirling beneath the surface.

Having said that, we should never push ourselves into territories that feel they may overwhelm us entirely, especially when our mental and emotional states may already be at their weakest. We do this work incrementally which means that we may cycle back through the same thoughts, feelings and fears many times as we address them at a deeper level each time. The healing expands and the load becomes lighter as we go. When feelings become too overwhelming, it is perfectly okay to take a step back and to take a break from this work until you feel ready to take another dive into it. If at any point you feel like you cannot safely approach this work on your own, I urge you to seek out the help of a mental health professional for added support as you begin this process, especially if you find yourself tending toward suicidal ideation. You may also seek the support of a trusted friend with whom you feel comfortable expressing your thoughts and emotions, if you prefer. We are not here to punish ourselves for being in pain, rather it is our goal that we may feel the feelings in order to reach the other side, a place of deep understanding, acceptance and love for ourselves.

No one who is on the path of healing and growth will tell you that it is easy. The rewards it offers, however, are incomparable. As we progress, we will discuss healthy ways to channel, process and release these feelings as we experience them. The reality is that the bulk of the transformative work is done simply in feeling the feeling itself. Oftentimes, the thoughts and emotions resolve themselves once we've had the courage to allow our inner selves to be heard by *feeling* what is there to be felt. There may be nothing more you need do.

Unfelt feelings do not simply go away. We are not dodging any bullets by avoiding them, even if it seems that way in the short term. Studies on the immediate and long-term effects of trauma on the body are ongoing and results are being continually interpreted. While the data compounds and ideologies about treatments are developed, there is significant evidence that the effects of trauma are made evident in physical, as well as mental and emotional, symptoms. The bad news is that trauma does impact the cells of the body and will likely continue to insidiously impact our lives for as long as it goes unaddressed. The good news is that I truly believe there are many ways and means of processing, healing and mitigating the effects of trauma. However, they all require dealing with it. Feeling our feelings—*without judgment*—is one of our first and foremost steps on this journey, and that act alone can have incomparable healing effects for our hearts, minds and bodies.

Regulating Your Nervous System

As we undergo the process of feeling our feelings and navigating life in recovery, learning to regulate the nervous system becomes ground zero for our healing work. Self-regulation tools help us to safely embark on this journey and provide much needed relief in times of upheaval or emotional intensity. Breath work is a low-key power player in trauma recovery. Learning to pay attention to your breath is a powerful tool for self-regulation. Breath is the gateway to suppressed emotions, blocked energy and the unconscious mind—all those hidden pockets of trauma that are tucked away in our bodies. Breathing may be the most essential and foundational tool in our day-to-day journey. Learning to harness the power of your breath so that it can work *for* you instead of against you is a power move.

We may not notice it, but in times of high intensity, humans instinctually hold their breath. Holding our breath is a subconscious way of holding back emotions and will, in fact, effectively help us to suppress them. Notice what happens next time you are trying *not* to cry. Invariably, you will find yourself holding your breath or breathing shallowly. In moments of tragedy, grief, shock, stress or danger, our bodies will commonly default to this tactic. It's as if holding our breath were some sort of subconscious attempt to control the external world when we feel a lack of such control.

When I first escaped cult life, I was seeing a (legitimate and licensed) counselor for a brief time who helped me to make the leap out of the cult and assisted me in the first few months of my transition back into mainstream society. She is the one who first instilled in me the idea that I may yet create a "life worth living," as Socrates posed, after a whole life lived under coercive control. One of the most impactful tools she offered me was a reminder of the importance of breathing, along with a specific breathing technique to calm my nervous system. I felt immediate results when I remembered to use this technique and so I began to use it as if my life depended on it. At times, it did.

Putting It Into Practice
A Breathing Exercise

Block breathing is a method for focusing on the breath through a specific breathing pattern in which you inhale, hold the breath, exhale and hold the breath all on the same count. For example, inhale on a four count, hold the breath for a four count, exhale on a four count and pause for a four count. Block breathing can assist with grounding, calming and focus.

For extra calming benefits, we can take this block breathing exercise and modify it with an extended exhale. This technique has been shown to bring the parasympathetic nervous system online which helps to calm and regulate our body and mind.

Try this technique for calming the nervous system and for general feel-good vibes:

- Breathe in fully through your nose, filling the belly and lungs completely, on a count of 4
- Hold your breath at that full capacity for a count of 4
- Exhale slowly through your mouth for a count of 8
- Repeat as needed

The key to this technique is that the exhale extends twice as long as the inhale. You can modify the timing however you please, with this ratio in mind, to experience the physically relieving benefits of lowered heart rate, decreased blood pressure and release of physical tension.

The counselor encouraged me to set a reminder on my phone that would go off several times a day to practice a mindfulness exercise which included noticing my breath. While the mindfulness exercise did not work for me at that time—mainly because it was too similar to practices I was compelled to do in the cult and therefore increased my anxiety—the aspect of remembering to notice my breath did help, and it stuck with me. In one of my first ever acts of choosing to listen to my own internal guidance above all others—even that of a mental health "authority"—I disposed of the part of the exercise that did not work for me and embraced the part that did. This specific breathing technique works to activate the vagus nerve (which makes up the bulk of the parasympathetic nervous system)[4] calming the mind and body in times of high anxiety or stress, which were common daily occurrences

---

[4] The autonomic nervous system (ANS) is responsible for regulating involuntary bodily functions, such as breathing, digestion, heart rate, sexual response, body temperature and blood pressure. The ANS has two sub-systems which play significant roles in regulating these bodily functions. The sympathetic nervous system is the branch of our ANS that is responsible for activating our fight-or-flight mode. The parasympathetic nervous system is the branch that is responsible for calming and relaxing our bodies, known as the rest-and-digest or the feed-and-breed response. The vagus nerve is a cranial nerve and it makes up about 75% of the parasympathetic nervous system. It is the only nerve in this system that runs from the brain down past our head all the way to our chest and belly, connecting to our heart, lungs and various vital organs. Bringing the parasympathetic nervous system back into balance with our overactive sympathetic nervous system is a critical component of trauma recovery. For a deeper dive, visit https://my.clevelandclinic.org/health/body/23266-parasympathetic-nervous-system-psns and https://www.mhs-dbt.com/blog/parasympathetic-nervous-system-and-trauma/.

for me.

Using this brief technique throughout the day, as needed, I could feel the calming effects in my body and mind. While it did not eradicate all anxiety and stress, I could feel a palpable shift as the tension in my body relaxed and the rate of my heart lowered every time I employed it. Sometimes the effects were more dramatic than others, but because it was so consistently impactful, I found myself coming back to the technique on a regular basis. As I did, I gradually came to notice and connect with my breath more and more. It afforded me a bit of space to think a little more clearly.

Taking deep breaths is a surefire way to ground yourself and calm the nervous system. For coping with C-PTSD, it is essential to learn healthy methods for regulating our emotions and nervous system. Breathing is one of the most basic forms of regulation we can employ. It can be done anywhere, at any time, without anyone even noticing. I encourage you to use this simple tool whenever you feel any kind of anxiety or distress.

In the practice of being still and learning to listen, breath is a necessary tool which will assist you greatly in the process. Notice your breath during these times. Remind yourself *to* breathe. Allow yourself to enjoy the deep inhales and exhales as you allow the thoughts and feelings hidden within you to rise to the surface. You can use your breath in this way to help open the door to stuck emotions or thoughts that you are ready to acknowledge and release. When you feel like there's nothing there within you to hear or feel, notice your breath and see if you are holding it or breathing shallow. If so, give some attention to deepening your breath, letting it flow freely, and check again.

Another reason these breathing practices are so helpful is that they require us to come into the present moment. Becoming present interrupts spinning thoughts and spiraling emotions that may threaten to overwhelm us and become counterproductive to this work. Another helpful regulating technique is to bring your focus to the immediate physical senses: notice the sensation of the fabric against your skin, take note of the colors you see in the environment around you and even name them out loud, notice the feeling of the ground beneath your feet or the seat beneath you. Concentrating on your immediate, physical surroundings and sensations can similarly serve to bring us into the present, calm the nervous system, and interrupt thoughts or feelings that threaten to become too intense.

When you do feel deep pockets of emotion surfacing, staying connected to your breath and the present moment will help to usher you safely through the process. Allow the feelings to surface. Acknowledge the thoughts behind them. Then let it out, let it flow and let it go. Allow the energy behind these painful feelings to move, move, move through and out of you. Breathe it out. Scream it out. Cry it out. Just *let it out*. This is the "work" of healing. This is one of the roads to freedom.

Honoring What You Hear & Feel

While we may automatically look for solutions and assistance when we are in a state of distress, I've found that learning to use these tools throughout the stable times, and even in the good times, makes them much more accessible during the hard times. It may even help to prevent some of the bad times as well. In fact, when these tools are needed most—when we are in distress, with mind racing, shallow-rapid breathing, heart pumping—is exactly when they can be hardest to pull out of our recovery toolkit because of the disorienting effect of heightened emotional or triggered states[5]. That's why it is essential to build in a little time to sit with yourself as early as possible in your recovery process. I'm fully aware of how uncomfortable this practice can be at first, which is why it is so helpful to gently and gradually cultivate your ability to attend to your own inner state in relatively calm times so that your ability to do so in triggered moments is greater.

Once you've done the hard work of sitting still, being quiet, listening to your heart and mind and focusing on your breath, the final step is to honor whatever comes up. The ultimate act of love, in this process, is to pay heed to the thoughts and feelings that arise and *act* on whatever needs you uncover there. If you need to give yourself permission to have a good cry, go ahead and bawl your eyes out.

Pete Walker is a therapist who specializes in C-PTSD. In his book, *Complex PTSD: From Surviving to Thriving,* Walker explains the science behind the therapeutic physical, mental and emotional effects of releasing tears. He calls it a "get-out-of-jail-free-card" for its tremendous impact in alleviating flashbacks, releasing stored pain and bringing our parasympathetic nervous system back online (just like our breathing technique does). Tears shed from emotional crying release chemicals,

---

[5] A trigger is an event or circumstance that sparks mental and/or emotional distress. It may be external, such as a sight, sound or smell, or internal, such as a thought, memory or physical sensation. The sound of a car backfiring may trigger a combat veteran with PTSD, as an example of an overt trigger. Other times, they may be much more subtle. Triggers elicit a reaction based on a previous experience of trauma; however, the connection between the trigger and the reaction may not always be clear. The reaction caused by a trigger can range from mild discomfort to extreme distress. Triggers are a common consequence of PTSD and C-PTSD. Learning to recognize when we have been triggered, and to manage triggers when they occur, is part of our self-regulation and healing process.

hormones and toxins, including both oxytocin and endorphins, which assist in calming and regulating physical and emotional pain. That's right; the very act of crying is a mental and emotional regulation tool. It can do wonders for transforming our internal and external state, both in the immediate and the long-term.

No matter what comes up, the important thing is to follow through with providing that outlet for yourself. It may not be tears that come up but a need to scream. Do it! If necessary, grab a pillow to scream into or let it out when you're alone in your car. Screaming has enormous therapeutic benefits as well. Other common internal responses may be a need to move (run, walk, jump up and down, shake out your arms and legs, dance—whatever you feel), stare into space allowing your mind to relax, sleep/rest, watch TV, laugh, or combine those last two and spend time watching a comedic movie or TV show. You may need something to soothe you, like some gentle music, a hot shower or bath, a calm stretching session, or completely escaping reality for a while through a good book. Maybe you need to feed yourself or drink a cool glass of water.

The more we listen and respond to what our body and heart are telling us, the easier it becomes to naturally tune into those needs and desires. The more quickly and easily we recognize and meet those needs, the more we are setting ourselves up for ultimate success, not just in the recovery process, but in everyday life. This process begins to rebuild those integral connections between our mind, body and spirit, leading to true healing.

In prolonged periods of trauma, we often forego even our most basic physical needs because we are running in survival mode and living in a state of hyper vigilance. During my time in the cult and while I was employed by the leader, I would commonly forego food, water and bathroom breaks due to the stressors and demands of my environment. I could not afford the time to step away for a bathroom break when I needed to, so I would hold it for hours until I could literally run to the restroom and then back to work as quickly as possible. Time constraints often impacted my ability to eat when I was hungry or to get some water when I was thirsty. Not only did my leader set impossible standards and assign enormous workloads to each employee to keep us continually overwhelmed and running ragged, but every corner of the stores in which I worked was monitored by video surveillance so he could watch our every move. The cameras recorded weeks' worth of footage at a time, so even if he didn't happen to be observing us in real time, he could and did review random moments from throughout the previous weeks, each one a new opportunity to find or create some wrongdoing for which we could be criticized, berated, ostracized, shunned, publicly humiliated or monetarily penalized. Occasionally, someone's employment itself would be threatened. I lived in a fishbowl and acted accordingly, in a state of constant hypervigilance, paranoia, and ceaseless action.

Further, my own body's needs were secondary to my leader's. I often had to defer my natural rhythm to match his, eating when he was ready to eat, eating what he wanted to eat, sleeping when he was ready to sleep and waking when he wanted to wake. This behavior not only served to further disconnect me from myself but reinforced my body's survival instincts, keeping me running in an endless "survival mode" both physically and psychologically.

I found that one of the simplest ways to initiate this practice of listening to myself on an ongoing basis was to start by eating when I was hungry, drinking when I was thirsty and stopping to go to the restroom whenever I felt the urge arise. As basic as that may sound, for many trauma survivors, this task alone can be daunting, due to how disconnected we have become from our own body-mind and its natural signals. This practice of tuning into and learning to identify these signals is important groundwork in the process of reconnecting with ourselves.

Make a point of paying attention to these three basic needs and fulfilling them on a daily, even hourly, basis. These are three of our most primal human needs. When the sympathetic nervous system perceives a threat and activates our fight-or-flight mode, it suppresses these basic impulses within the body to prioritize survival while one of the "Four Fs" (fight, flight, freeze or fawn) takes over. Therefore, when we consistently ignore or postpone the fulfillment of these basic human functions, we are signaling to our bodies and minds that it is necessary to continue operating in survival mode. Essentially, we are telling ourselves that we are not safe because we cannot afford to eat, drink and eliminate when necessary.

As you begin to practice being still, listening to yourself and decoding your body's and mind's messages, do your very best to honor what you learn by putting action behind it. You may not always have the means or ability to indulge the needed action in that moment, but if not, make a plan for how you can give yourself what you're needing, and make sure to create a timeline for when you can fulfill that need. As we practice suspending judgment of ourselves in this process, our courage and commitment to do this healing work naturally increases.

It is so, so important that, when we spend this time sitting quietly with ourselves and listening to what we're feeling and thinking, we treat ourselves with the same open-mindedness, tenderness and attentiveness that we would someone else for whom we cared deeply and who required our help. I encourage you to approach this time much the way you would if your closest, dearest and most beloved friend were confiding in you with her innermost thoughts. Rarely would we regard someone else's raw, open vulnerability with the same harshness with which we are apt to approach ourselves. If you have been guilty of this double-standard toward yourself, it's time to change your ways. When you listen to your innermost thoughts and feelings, step outside of yourself and frame the experience as if it *were* your best friend confiding in you. After all, *it is*.

Mistakes: Moving From Inner Critic to Inner Cheerleader

We all have that inner critic voice in our heads and it loves to get mouthy when we make mistakes. And we *all* make mistakes, by the way. Not only are mistakes human, but they are a necessary part of our growth process. At their highest, mistakes are lessons, but I know better than anyone how difficult it can be to accept that concept.

Although my group's leader loved to proclaim the importance of mistakes and that they are nothing more than "lessons unlearned, revisited once again," he would also be the first to condemn, berate, humiliate or punish one of us when we made one. Worse yet, he would actively seek them out, and on countless occasions, created mistakes where none actually existed, a common tactic among narcissists. My relationship with mistakes was already precarious, after a childhood in which my parents were all too eager to implement the precept of "spare the rod, spoil the child" through corporal punishment. Spoiled, my sister and I were not. Terrified of any potential misstep for fear of that not-lightly-applied leather belt, we certainly were.

My time in the cult doubled down on my deeply instilled fear around mistakes. By the time I got out, my body had developed a well-rehearsed panic response to mistakes. My heart would skip a beat (or two) and then start racing. My face flushed. A flash of heat would course through my body, creating prickly stings around my face, neck and underarms. My breathing became shallow or ceased altogether. I braced myself for the punishment, berating, condemnation or conflict to come. As a result of all this conditioning, my inner critic was *fierce*.

Learning to shut down my inner voice of judgment is the kindest, most loving act I have ever undertaken for myself. Now that I am free, there is no one left to berate and torture me but myself. I discovered that, although I learned this habit well, it was not actually natural to me. I did not enjoy accusing and condemning myself, nor did I find it helpful in my learning and growth.

Mistakes are going to happen. They are part of life. But the inner critic doesn't have to be. Now is a good time to cultivate a practice of recognizing the inner critic when it is speaking to you. It is important to begin to recognize that voice and that it is not *your* natural voice. It is a voice that is unique to each of us, but it is not innate, we are not born with it. It is formulated from our past, our conditioning, former authority figures and the voices of those whom we have feared the most. If you pay close enough attention, you may even be able to identify whose voice it really is.

Step one, recognize. Step two, replace.

When I make a mistake now, especially if it is work-related, my body still has its rehearsed panic response. However, the severity of that reaction is steadily decreasing and I am optimistic for a day when it is negligible. This has taken practice, however, and I must be consistent in applying the antidote when these incidences occur.

One of the first things I remind myself is to *breathe*. Focusing on my breath opens up space in my mind where clarity can enter. I then begin to speak kindly, gently and lovingly to myself, reassuring myself. This is my job now, since I am my own protector and greatest advocate. When the harsh, critical voice arises, I must firmly dismiss it. Then, I purposefully speak to myself with compassion, understanding and empathy. What I say to myself will vary according to the specifics of the situation, but it will be something along the lines of:

> *It is just a mistake. I will do what I can to fix it. I will take responsibility for it. I will make amends, if necessary. I do not deserve to be ridiculed or punished. I will use this to learn and grow. You are safe and I love you. This does not make you bad. You are still good and you are still loved.*

I am also speaking to the scared little girl deep inside me. Practice speaking kindly to yourself at *all* times—from when you first see your reflection in the mirror in the morning to when you've indulged in that second pint of Ben & Jerry's to when you receive a word of praise—and you will fast-track your inner critic replacement, transforming it into your inner cheerleader. You deserve to be spoken to with love, and if you don't set that precedent for yourself, how will you uphold that standard for others in relationship with you?

A Note On Inner Child Work

I first encountered the concept of inner child work when I was already well within the grips of the high-control group. Awareness and popularity of this concept has grown tremendously since that time, especially in the context of those healing from childhood traumas and/or relationships with emotionally immature or abusive parents. Inner child work involves reconnecting with your heart and mind from your earliest years of life and not only befriending that little one, but also gently, kindly re-parenting him or her. The thoughts and feelings of that scared, isolated or stuck little child are often quietly informing our way of being as adults, without us even realizing it.

I don't know about you, but the first time I heard about doing "inner child work," I felt queasy. It made me uncomfortable. It seemed silly, new age-y and woo-woo. That's right, even for someone who was committed to a spirituality-and-therapy-based high control group! I never felt particularly comfortable around children and certainly didn't feel any sense of childlikeness in myself. I'd learned to behave and appear as a little adult from an incredibly young age, and I simply didn't have any sense of an inner child within myself.

However, when the conditions I was immersed in were rapidly increasing in cultic intensity, the life coach/leader steered me in the direction of a therapeutic self-guided workbook which combined mirror work techniques and inner child work. These techniques can help to reconnect us with parts of ourselves we've buried or disconnected from for self-protective purposes, and it can feel uncomfortable and awkward at first. Being the ever-diligent student and follower that I was, I worked my way through the program from start to finish, pushing past my aversions and unearthing some deep-seated pain. This was just one of the many critical tools that were presented that helped me to save myself while I was still trapped under a cultic control that, at the very same time, manipulated other spiritual and self-help concepts to keep me paralyzed and stuck. Even so, while doing that powerful work, I connected with a part of myself that I had never been in touch with before, and I have retained that connection to some degree ever since. I credit that work with being a vital asset in not losing myself completely in the cult and with initiating a practice of self-love and self-protection that would ultimately help me to break free.

The trauma-recovery and reconnection-to-self process necessarily involves our inner child. For those of us who have lost that connection, learning to hear our inner child, love our inner child, protect and care for our inner child and re-parent our inner child is at the root level of reconnecting with ourselves and learning to love ourselves. While I am not qualified to teach or coach anyone through that process, I can attest to the benefit of doing this type of work. There are many excellent resources that *can* guide you through a deep dive of inner child healing exercises and I highly recommend that you check them out if you feel so inspired. It may be worth exploring if you feel disconnected from this aspect of yourself. Most of us who experienced childhood trauma have some deep work available to do in this area and it can be intensely healing for us.

3

Intuition: Honing Your Hidden Superpower

Every single human being possesses intuition. Intuition is that which is often referred to as a "sixth sense," and that is because it actually is our sixth sense. However, since intuition is unlike the other five senses we rely on to our navigate our world, in that it is considered a *nonphysical* sense, it may be disregarded as illegitimate by some or nonexistent by others.

I believe that intuition is just as real and concrete as any of our other senses and it may be one of the most important. I believe that intuition is the link that ties together our physical and nonphysical selves, from our bodies to our minds to our spirits. However, just as some may experience limitations within a physical sense (I.e.: poor eyesight or hard of hearing), so do some experience a disconnect from their intuition. Nonetheless, we *all* have the capacity to tap into, hone and develop our intuitive sixth sense, if and when we choose. We are all already using it throughout our day, often without being aware it is what we are leaning on to navigate our world.

The reason intuition is so critical is because it is constantly attempting to steer us toward that which is good, safe and right for us. While it may not be considered a "physical" sense, we actually do experience this sense in our bodies in a variety of ways. Learning to tune into your intuitive senses, like tuning into a specific radio station, may be one of the most important ways we can learn to protect ourselves and to help others. As we begin to sit and listen to ourselves more and more, it will become easier to hear our innate intuition speaking to us through our inner voice.

We sometimes hear incredible stories of folks who evaded near disaster because they "heard a voice" or "had a feeling" that guided them to take an action which ended up saving their life or someone else's. This is just one example of intuition, on the grander scale, but it is typically more subtle. It is the sense that is guiding us through our every day, whether we are consciously aware of it or not. The more aware of it we become, however, the more we can use this sense to help us navigate our days and guide us toward positive, beneficial outcomes.

If you're among those who are reading this with doubt, or feeling that you may have gotten shafted on this sense when it was being handed out, I am here to tell you: Yes, *you too* have an inner voice, even if you don't think you hear it much yet. The more you listen to it, the louder and clearer it will get.

Follow the Breadcrumbs

To learn to consciously employ our intuition, we must first increase our sensitivity to it. The first step toward developing your intuition is to honor what you hear, see, feel or sense. There are many ways that our intuition speaks to us. Sometimes it is through a "gut feeling," other times it may be through images you see in your mind, a voice you hear in your mind (which may simply occur as an out-of-the-blue thought rather than a literal voice), or it may be a sudden conviction that you just *know* something. It can also be any combination of these experiences. Regardless of how intuition speaks to you, one of the best ways to increase your connection to it is, first, by paying attention and making note of what you're sensing, and second, by honoring that sense.

For example, if you're on your way out the door and you suddenly have an inspiration to turn around and grab your raincoat—even though you haven't looked at the weather yet—then do it. How many times have you said, or heard someone else say, "Aw man, I *knew* I should have (fill in the blank)"? When we don't listen to our intuition, we usually experience anything from a minor inconvenience to a major misfortune. This is not because we are being punished for not listening to it, it's just the natural occurrence resulting from that which our intuition was trying to warn us of.

Honoring these tiny intuitive impulses will help us to notice them more frequently. As we begin to notice them more frequently, we can begin to honor them more frequently. The more we honor them, the more we can experience the benefits, the assistance and the protection that our intuition is offering us.

One of the reasons I believe developing intuition is a critical part of our healing process is because it is *your* intuition that will guide you to the resources, methods and tools that *you* most need in your unique healing journey. For those of us recovering from complex trauma, narcissistic relationships and coercive control, reconnecting with our intuition is essential to rediscovering our true selves and preventing ourselves from finding our way back into those circumstances ever again. Our intuition is a great asset when we actively engage it.

In retrospect, I can pinpoint many times that my intuition was screaming at me during my years under cultic control. I can remember the twisted feeling in my gut as I went against the voice of my intuition to instead honor the wishes and demands of the leader. For years, I lived with the dire consequences of ignoring that intuition. I suffered greatly, and all the while, my intuition continued to attempt to help me. Had I been able to listen to that voice above all others, and *honor the guidance it was offering me* above the approval of the leader and beyond the fear instilled by what I was being told externally, I could have been spared some of that suffering. That is why I am now committed to using my hard-earned lessons to hear and honor my intuition to the best of my ability.

At the same time, I was also actively using my intuition to help me navigate the extremely precarious circumstances of day-to-day life with a malignant narcissist. You see, intuition is impartial. It does not judge us and it does not withdraw its assistance when we fail to heed its voice. It continues to quietly offer guidance.

As a child, I instinctively developed my intuitive and empathic senses to a high degree, because they enabled me to move more safely through my world. I became intensely aware of the ever-changing moods and energy of those around me. This enabled me to adjust accordingly, whether to more safely position myself, or in many cases, to avoid or mitigate negative consequences altogether. Many childhood trauma survivors instinctually develop these techniques, combined with a hypervigilance that never shuts off, which assist them in navigating and coping in a dangerous environment.

As an adult in the cultic group, these intuitive skills were extremely handy. They helped me to once again discern the ever-shifting mood of the leader and to tap into the best ways to alter myself or my surroundings to offer the most protection in any given moment. This tactic of coping became second nature to me, so I was truly baffled by others in close proximity to the leader who would barrel right through their world without any awareness of his shifting emotional tides, resulting in enormous turmoil or conflict that could have been easily avoided with a more heightened awareness. I then realized, for the first time, that not everyone is actively aware of these subtle energies. This realization helped me to recognize the ongoing gift that intuition is always offering us. It is available to us to the degree that we are willing to get quiet and listen to it. Even while I was unable to listen and honor that inner voice as I acted against it, being drawn further and further into the cultic quagmire, it was still actively assisting me to move through my world and survive it. Though this ability stemmed from unfortunate roots, I consider that heightened intuition to be a hidden treasure from my childhood, and we all have the ability to tap into it and develop it.

I still don't always get it right, though, and I still suffer when I overlook it or choose to actively ignore it. I'm still learning to trust that inner sense above all others and to use it for my greatest good. When I do pay attention to it and honor the guidance it is offering me with my actions, I invariably experience the benefits. Sometimes, that may be as simple as not getting soaked during an unexpected rainstorm. At other times, it has spared me from people, places and situations that would have been harmful to me.

We don't always get to see the immediate effects of listening to our intuition, as in the example of the raincoat, but oftentimes, we will find out much further down the road why our intuition was steering us in a specific way. It takes trust in ourselves to listen and honor what we feel, even when there is no immediate evidence for it. The more we honor it, the easier it will be for us to hear and *listen* to that guidance in the future.

Coming Back to Yourself

The most effective way to develop your intuition is to actively engage it. While it is important to pay attention so that you can notice and hear it when it arises in you, you don't have to wait for this to randomly occur. You can practice hearing your intuition by consciously tuning into it. This is where your time spent learning to be still and listen to yourself will reach its full potential.

In those still and quiet times, begin to ask yourself, "What am I feeling?" Give yourself the necessary time and space for the answer to arrive—for *all* the answers to arrive. More often than not, you may find that not only do you have a variety of different feelings, but some of them may be outright conflicting with one another. You may have a variety of different desires surfacing, and those, too, may be in direct conflict with one another. The initial stage of this process is not to judge any of the thoughts or feelings, nor is it to resolve the conflicts. It's purely an information gathering session.

The act of allowing your feelings to be felt may, in fact, alter what you are feeling. It may alter your perception of what you're feeling. It may give you new clarity about what you are experiencing in your body, mind or life. It is an act of love and kindness toward yourself—just to allow your feelings to be.

Once you have given yourself this grace, without judgment, you can elicit the help of your intuition. It is one of the simplest things in the world to do. You now turn to your inner self and ask, "What do you need?"

And listen.

There is no right or wrong answer here. There is no right or wrong way through the process. The answer may come in the form of something physical, it may be an action to take, or it may be something immaterial.

I have received answers ranging from "Chocolate" to "To be alone" to "Sleep" to "A conversation with that person" to "stillness." Sometimes, I am not able to provide for myself the thing I need. It may be out of my grasp in that moment or out of my control altogether. Nonetheless, being aware of it helps me to navigate it, and wherever possible, to find creative alternatives that may offer an effective substitute.

Whatever you hear in response to your questions, honor it to the best of your ability. Just the act of hearing and acknowledging the need within yourself can be profoundly healing. So many of us struggling with C-PTSD have foregone our own needs for so long in the service of survival and of others that we don't even know what they are anymore. The simple act of recognizing and acknowledging your personal needs is so important to reconnecting with yourself.

Whenever it is possible, and where it is healthy and safe to do so, take action to fulfill your own needs. Even if it can't be done in that moment, create an action plan to fulfill that need when it is possible.

**Please note here the difference between wants and needs. Unhealthy *wants*, when strong enough, can present themselves as *needs*. If you are someone who has struggled with substance abuse, for example, you may already know what this feels like. We must be gentle and honest with ourselves in discerning the difference and taking appropriate actions to fulfill our needs in a way that is healthy and loving to ourselves. It is also appropriate to find healthy ways to fulfill our *wants* whenever possible, as well.

I find that this is a prime time for my inner child to speak up. She is fun and spontaneous and loves all the cushy, comforting, good things in life. She does not want to experience limit or restriction in any way. She just wants to indulge and enjoy, to revel in all the good and beautiful and fun things in life. I love her; she is great. However, it is also my responsibility to look out for her and make sure that my long-term best interests are also served.

So, feel your feelings, hear your needs, and practice taking care of *yourself*. That is your primary function and responsibility in this healing and recovery journey. And if that statement is triggering all sorts of discomfort in you and telling you how selfish that is, please listen to that discomfort and let it have its say. But also, please understand that until we learn to truly care for ourselves, we won't be able to fully care for, or responsibly give to, others. Perhaps most importantly, if we don't learn to truly care for ourselves, *we are far more likely to turn to others to fulfill those needs within us*. Doing so can set us up for further exploitation, creating opportunity for unhealthy people, relationships and situations to enter our lives. This is a danger for any human being, but for those struggling to regain their life and footing with C-PTSD, this is an especial danger.

Repetition

The key to mastering any skill is repetition. To hone our intuition, whether it's new to us or something we've relied on our whole lives, we need to do it over and over again. In order to get good at hearing and following our intuition, we have to practice using it.

A lot of the time, we learn to hear our intuition by experiencing the results of *not* listening to it. Pain is a great teacher. If we pay attention, we can often find our intuition's earlier guidance in the sentiment, "I *should* have (fill in the blank)."

Rather than beating ourselves up over the missed opportunity, we can use that as a new opportunity to take note within ourselves of how the intuition showed up. Even though we failed to honor it this time, half the battle is learning to recognize it in the first place. Now, we're presented with a brand-new opportunity to learn how that intuition was showing up for us and thereby increasing our chances of noticing it the next time. Once again, we will get better at this through repetition, so go ahead and accept that you're probably going to miss those signals sometimes, and when you do, you'll get a better understanding of how those messages are showing up for you.

It is equally important that we give credence and attention to all the times that we *do* hear and honor our intuition. This will also help us to hone in on it and listen more closely moving forward. When the rain starts pouring and you have your raincoat to put on, that is worth a big ol' pat on the back. When you hear the phone ring and take a moment to stop and discern who is on the other end before you see the caller's name, that is you actively engaging your intuition. Acknowledge yourself for getting it right.

If you found yourself plopped down in the middle of a dark forest all alone, having never been there before, it would take time for you to learn to navigate your way through it. You wouldn't expect to know where to go or the fastest route to the closest water source or what direction to turn for the nearest town, right out of the gate. Your steps might be timid at first and you would likely travel in circles at times. However, with practice and time, the terrain becomes more familiar and you begin to recognize landmarks within the vast space. Spend enough time in that forest and it will become a familiar space, perhaps even with a sense of home.

The most important thing you can do is to just keep practicing. Keep paying attention. Keep honoring your inner voice when you're able to hear it clearly. And keep taking note of the results, one way or the other. The more attention you give to it, the easier the process will become. The end result is that your intuition can become a well-built muscle on which you come to steadfastly rely for clear guidance in times of fear, doubt and need.

A Note On Your Badassery

Doing this healing and recovery work is far more heroic than society will give you credit for, but those of us who have been there in it, like you, know just how incredible a feat it is. Learning to care for ourselves, to be responsible in our actions and reactions to others, learning to truly listen to and honor our intuition, and doing the grueling work of becoming a healthy, balanced person from the inside out, is probably the most impressive accomplishment anyone can achieve.

As badly as we may want it to, **it does not happen overnight.** In my mind, it is right up there with Olympic Gold Medal status because it requires a similar level of dedication, discipline, pain, repetition, commitment, sweat, tears and hard work to accomplish. I am fully convinced, however, that it is the single most rewarding, satisfying and worthwhile thing we can commit our lives to.

To top it all off, most of us are doing this work *on top of* full time jobs, familial commitments, and/or all of the other full-time day-to-day duties and obligations that are required to simply live and survive in this world. To say that it can be overwhelming is an understatement. You who are committing yourself to this work—you are truly a hero and I acknowledge you for this incredible task to which you have dedicated yourself. Remember to acknowledge yourself, as well.

4

The Body & Basic Survival

When I got out, my body was a wreck. I do not have a word for the level of exhaustion I felt, but despite that, I couldn't sleep for more than four to five hours. I was finally free to eat whatever I wanted and whenever I wanted, but my body didn't seem to be absorbing nutrients. My digestive system was in upheaval. No matter how healthy the meal I consumed, my stomach churned and strained to process it. I was flooded with emotional energy and I didn't know what to do with it. For the first time in my life, long-suppressed anger rose to the surface and I felt unadulterated rage coursing through my veins. I wanted to hit something. I instinctively knew that's exactly what I needed to do.

Each one of these aspects required its own time and attention to address: sleep, nutrition, exercise and emotional release. I grappled with each aspect to the degree that I was capable at any given time. I sought out resources and assistance, doing my research along the way, for the aspects in which I felt completely lost.

I quickly began to learn just how connected my mind, body and heart truly are. While I conceptualized this idea in my years of culty self-help work, the experience of it became very real in my day-to-day recovery life. In the group, all emphasis was put on the "spiritual," forgoing the mental and physical aspects almost entirely. There was no true integration of these dynamically interwoven elements and that was on purpose, because it served to impair our critical thinking abilities keeping us mired in the group's indoctrination.

In these groups, critical thinking is strongly discouraged, and in my case, I was often told that I relied too much on my intellect. I was labeled an over thinker. I was admonished to stop trying to "figure things out" because that was just my ego keeping me detained in the mental realm. By instilling a powerful sense of guilt, this approach stopped me from questioning and challenging my situation and circumstances too deeply. In turn, that tactic kept the leader in a position of unchallenged power. Finally, it provided an easy out when I asked questions that the leader did not have answers for. I might hear, "Stop resorting to your intellect, Christina. You can't 'think' your way out of this!" in response to some question I posed about the path of spiritual enlightenment. End of conversation. I experienced the same thought-stopping approaches in the radical evangelicalism of my youth. Different ideologies, but the same thought-stopping outcomes.

What's more, bodies were considered virtually irrelevant in our group, up until the last few years. (The leader would later change his approach on this topic, when it served his exploitative interests to do so.) Bodies were seen as mere vehicles to cart us around on the physical plane and deserved no real attention, we were taught. Preoccupation with the body was yet another ego attachment and ego derailment from our spiritual pursuits. Attempts to "look good" (by wearing makeup, fixing your hair, focusing on clothing or jewelry) were, at times, condemned as egoic ploys to seduce others. One member who is naturally athletic was strongly dissuaded from engaging in regular exercise because it was deemed no more than an attempt to glorify and overemphasize the body. As a result, I learned to all but completely ignore my body, giving no attention to appearance, health, nutrition, exercise or physical well-being.

Once I got out, it became apparent to me that, to truly heal on any level, I must address my issues on *every* level. However, the extent to which I am capable of addressing a particular area varies throughout the recovery journey and will often flow from one area to another as I go along. Physical health became an early priority in my first months of recovery, out of necessity. However, I quickly learned that my physical well-being was deeply impacted by my emotional state and vice versa. As I experienced small amounts of healing in my body, my mental and emotional health were positively impacted as well. This is just one of the reasons why learning to be still and to listen to myself is so crucial along this path, so that I can respond appropriately to the areas that most need my attention and to pivot as those needs shift.

Dissociation and Somatic Healing

Dissociation and disassociation are common among trauma survivors. While not exactly the same, these terms are often used interchangeably in the world of recovery. "Dissociation is an involuntary experience that occurs when you feel disconnected from yourself or your environment. Disassociation…is a conscious separation or detachment from something or someone and can be a coping mechanism" (https://www.webmd.com/mental-health/dissociation-overview).

The experience of trauma is one of the common causes of dissociation, which includes the experience of feeling disconnected from one's body, detached from others or emotions, not feeling real or as if the world is not real, emotional numbness, mental fog, racing heart with lightheadedness, feeling as if you are someone else and "spacing out"—just to name a few. These symptoms can range from mild to extreme degrees of manifestation, the more extreme being dissociative identity disorder (previously known as multiple personality disorder). The experience of dissociation may vary widely and uniquely for each individual.

In my experience, dissociation has been both a consequence of trauma and a coping mechanism during trauma. I unknowingly began to experience intense symptoms of dissociation in my early teenage years as a consequence of childhood trauma. Hours-long "space out" sessions in which I escaped the world of reality were common for me as a teenager, for example. I have grappled with many of these dissociative symptoms to varying degrees and intensities throughout my life.

I likewise discovered the power of *disassociation* as a coping mechanism at a very young age. I clearly remember the last beating with a belt I received in which I first consciously employed this technique. The punishment was for talking back to my father. This was simply not done in my household and disagreement with him would result in a fierce reminder of his authority. In a rare show of rebellion on this day, however, I did not care. I was enraged because I'd learned that a new friend of mine was likely being sexually abused in her home and I went to my parents in full confidence that something would be done, with no knowledge or care for the intricacies of intervening in these matters. When I discovered that no action was going to be taken, I was furious. I heatedly contested this verdict by angrily talking back.

I was indignant that my Gospel-spouting preacher of a father would take no action against this injustice. When I was beaten with a belt for this insolence, I wore the fire of my fury like a shield and I steeled my mind against the moment by first determining that I would not cry and secondly by disconnecting from my body during those humiliating and painful moments. The tactic worked and I learned the power of my own mind to alter my experience of reality.

So many of us have defaulted to dissociation to cope with our environments and our lack of control over what was happening to, or around, us. This tactic, while necessary at that time, creates a divide between our heart, mind and body which can lead to many other chronic issues and symptoms. Healing this rupture by learning to once again inhabit the bodies in which we live is a crucial aspect of healing from trauma. It is about discovering that we are actually safe now, safe in our own bodies, safe in our habitat, safe in the world. It doesn't mean that we will never use these coping mechanisms again, but we can learn to recognize them and to exert greater control over when and how we use them. This is a process which takes time and space to evolve, but we *can* begin to train our bodies and our minds to relax and experience a sense of safety in the present, instead.

When I was in my darkest years of cultic control, my body was repeatedly placed in situations which I *hated*...but which I felt I had no power over. Since I felt I had no control over my physical reality at those times, I used my mind to escape it through disassociation, just as I'd organically discovered how to do as a child. I automatically detached myself mentally and emotionally for the sake of preventing uncontrollable physical outbursts that otherwise threatened to break loose from within me. Disassociation was the only tool I had, at that time, to cope with the situation, and it was absolutely necessary in order for me to mentally and emotionally survive the circumstances within which I lived.

This dissociative tendency not only resulted in a deep rift between my inner self and my body (forget trying to love your body when you don't even inhabit it!), but it also caused a disconnect between my mind and my emotions. Each one of these divides has to be gradually repaired with gentle loving-kindness toward ourselves. One of the pleasanter surprises I have discovered is that each bit of repair I manage to do on one of these rifts, such as my connection to my body, will flow out and support the repair of the other two, such as my mental and emotional well-being. Just as they all had to disconnect from one another in trauma-survival-mode, they all naturally want to come back into full connection with one another in the healing process. Reconnecting to our bodies through somatic healing processes is just one aspect in this trinity of our true selves.

The *Psychology Today* website explains,

> *Somatic therapy is a form of body-centered therapy that looks at the connection of mind and body and uses both psychotherapy and physical therapies for holistic healing. In addition to talk therapy, somatic therapy practitioners use mind-body exercises and other physical techniques to help release the pent-up tension that negatively affects a patient's physical and emotional well-being (https://www.psychologytoday.com/us/therapy-types/somatic-therapy).*

Somatic healing—this process of releasing the stuck or stored energy, resulting from trauma, within our bodies—is a critical component of healing our hearts, minds *and* bodies. As trauma survivors, we come to live the experience of how irrevocably connected all these parts of ourselves actually are. The fragmentation that we experience through our trauma, and the resulting coping mechanisms, often lead to severe mental and physical health issues, even once we're long removed from the traumatic space, because its effects are so deep and long lasting. However, I wholeheartedly believe it is possible to mitigate, and maybe even prevent, some of those long-term effects through conscious healing and recovery work. Although I did not have the opportunity to work with a somatic healing practitioner when I first got out, I found my own means of employing somatic healing techniques.

One of the first issues I addressed, due to its alarming intensity, was the emotional storm of rage in my body that clearly needed somewhere to go. I purchased a punching bag, and with the help of friends, filled the base with sand, set it in the corner of a garage and began to wail on it regularly. I didn't have the energy or strength to punch and kick for very long, but that didn't matter. That wasn't the point. The point was to move the overwhelming emotional energy trapped in my body and release it out of me. I pushed the energy out with every punch and every kick and that bag willingly absorbed it. The tables had turned; no longer was I the one taking the hits but the one delivering them. This symbolic shift also delivered a subtle sense of empowerment. Sometimes I cried as I wailed on the bag. Occasionally I screamed. Always, I played very loud, heavy metal rock music to shroud my energetic releases.

The punching bag was a crucial first step in what became a form of somatic healing. It gave me a healthy outlet to direct my rage and release the buried pockets of fury, grief and depression that I had been holding back for so long. The vibrational impact of kicking and punching the bag moved those pockets of energy through my body allowing some of it to be released. The empowering side effect of beating on the bag like a badass helped to mend my mind and heart as well.

I also began to recognize the gift of anger. When channeled properly, the power and strength that anger provides can serve to protect us. Anger helps us to identify when our boundaries have been threatened or crossed. When I was punished for expressing my anger and speaking back to my father, it was just one of countless times in my life that I was taught to hold my tongue, suppress my rage and comply...*or else.* I was taught that anger was an unacceptable response and a dangerous emotion for me to have. I learned to suppress it, and by the time I reached adulthood, I rarely felt it at all. However, it was also my rage that helped to protect me from the physical pain that resulted from the beating, and I now realize that anger can protect me from so much more.

When I broke free from the group and began beating on a punching bag, it was the first time in my life I allowed myself to freely feel, express and process barrels of long-suppressed anger and rage. I was terrified, at first. I feared these emotions would overwhelm and consume me. I had always shied away from them as unspiritual and unenlightened aspects. I also observed how my group's leader was ruled by these emotions and stood by helplessly while he used them unabashedly to bully me and others. Therefore, I associated these emotions with destruction and meanness. Not least, in our culture, women are strongly discouraged from expressing any anger at all, and we are often dismissed as "hysterical" or "ugly" when we do. All of these deterrents had hidden from me the power and protection that anger, as a natural and healthy response to crossed boundaries, is intended to provide. While anger can be a dangerous weapon when brandished irresponsibly, it also holds important information for us, and I learned that I should respect and honor this response when it arises in me.

Of course, there were physical benefits for my body that accompanied the emotional release. My long-unused cardiac system began to gradually increase in strength, enabling me to lengthen my kickboxing sessions by a minute or two at a time. My arms and legs started to get stronger and I could see the slightest bit of tone coming back into my muscles. But my purpose was really to strengthen my sanity, emotional health and overall well-being. Focusing on that purpose kept me motivated to return to the bag several days a week and prevented me from making any judgments about "progress." If I kick boxed for only five minutes and that was all I could do, that was enough, because it was one more day of healthy emotional release. The more I could free my mind, heart and body of this pent-up energy, the better my chances of enjoying prolonged sleep, as well.

The counselor I saw when I first got out strongly encouraged me to consider incorporating yoga into my day-to-day routine, because of its known benefits for calming and resetting the central nervous system—a reset my body required. Once I'd moved some initial waves of trapped energy out of my system, I began to feel more drawn to the calmer practice of yoga. I dabbled with it at home via free YouTube videos.

When I was about nine months free, I decided to investigate a hot yoga studio near where I lived. I was greatly intimidated by the idea of taking my novice-level yoga ability into an actual studio and practicing in front of other people, but I finally worked up the courage. I quickly fell in love. I found another healthy release for moving more energy through my body, which invariably resulted in greater calm. The effect on my nervous system was transformative.

Before I knew it, I'd developed an intense passion for hot yoga. My body and mind craved it like a healthy drug. It provided such a physical challenge that my mind was forced to concentrate only on the task at hand (not falling over!), leaving the worries of the world behind, while continued waves of emotional energy found space to move through my body and be sweated out.

Having said that, I would like to add a word of caution here regarding yoga. While a consistent yoga practice can do wonders for one's mind, body, and emotional health, I would be remiss not to point out that there are many unhealthy and high-control yoga groups. In fact, this can be true for a number of different exercise modalities, so it is important to be discerning and particular about where you choose to participate in these activities. Any group—yogic or otherwise—that compels you to follow, submit, or defer to a leader, or that attempts to assert control over you through strict rules and regulations, is a red flag. Finding a sense of camaraderie and community is great as long as it doesn't become manipulative, coercive, or controlling. Please go in with your eyes open and remember to do only what feels good and right for you, your body, and your life.

Finding your own forms of release is an important aspect of healing. It may not be yoga, but there is something that your body craves and that will calm your mind and nerves. Taking walks, for example, is a simple and highly effective mode of exercise for releasing tension, gaining mental clarity and providing emotional decompression. The natural bilateral stimulation of our arm, leg and eye movements while walking can have a similar impact on our minds, emotions and nervous system; this is the basis of the specialized trauma therapy known as EMDR (eye movement desensitization and reprocessing). This therapy uses a system of bilateral stimulation during the recollection of traumas to help the individual reprocess the experience(s) and reduce the mental and emotional stress caused by them. Just the simple act of going for a walk can itself provide a similar effect as we work to process and release the mental, emotional and physical stress from trauma throughout our healing journey. Our bodies want to move and our minds want to calm. Be willing to tap into a sense of curiosity, openness and exploration to discover the path that works best for *your* body-mind.

It could be running, swimming, martial arts, dancing, stretching, jumping up and down, or any other activity that releases energy. Lying on a bed kicking and screaming into a pillow can be a wonderful release! All that matters is that you are being as present as possible with yourself during the activity and that you allow whatever emotions that come up to be released in whatever way feels right: crying, laughing, screaming, moaning, and deep breathing are all examples of how that energy might be released in combination with the physical activity that is moving the energy through, and out of, the body.

Engaging in this practice consistently will help to expedite the process. The more often and more routinely we allow ourselves to go through this practice, the more release we're likely to experience in these early stages of recovery. So, jump on it any and every time you have the thought or impulse to do so! Consider it an act of love toward yourself and a kind gift for your heart, mind and body.

Prioritizing Rest

A second crucial aspect to trauma recovery is *rest*. This includes, but is not limited to, sleep. Unfortunately, this critical component often seems the most elusive of them all. It goes against every bit of training, teaching and conditioning we have received in our cultic, abusive and/or traumatizing living situations.

Coming out of long-term traumatic situations means that our minds and bodies have been on high alert for a very long time, pumping out high doses of adrenaline and releasing cortisol in alarming amounts. This is because we have been living in a state of "fight or flight," the state in which the body prepares itself for an intense survival encounter through either confronting (fighting) the threat or escaping (fleeing) it. The body is not intended to stay in this state indefinitely.

For example, the essential process our body and mind undergo in order to survive an unexpected encounter with a grizzly bear in the wild is not meant to *continue,* day in and day out, without ceasing. But that is exactly what happens when we are living in trauma-survival mode. The cortisol, the adrenaline, the tension and the hyper-alertness stay at their command stations, pumping out fight or flight readiness at all times. The wear and tear our minds and bodies suffer in the process is substantial.

Living in this mode does extensive damage to our nervous system and to the natural hormonal balance of our bodies, which inevitably leads to a cacophony of daily and long-term health issues. Calming the nervous system, bringing down the cortisol levels coursing through the veins and gradually restoring balance to the body's internal systems, especially our hormones, are critical aspects of recovery. While sound sleep and deep rest are essential for our minds and bodies at this time, I found these to be elusive flights of fancy in the early days of recovery. This experience seems to be common for trauma survivors and often a point of frustration.

Operating without sufficient sleep, unfortunately, can compound many of the other issues with which we are already grappling as survivors, so I strongly feel that addressing this issue, for those who are chronically keyed up and under-rested, is essential to the success of their recovery and healing process. Therefore, I believe it is one of the most urgent and serious issues to address when coming out of high trauma or ongoing trauma. Many of the sections in this book will offer suggestions that will be relevant to creating healthy sleep, rest and bedtime routines.

While I don't believe there is any miracle cure for this, my personal preference was not to opt for any pharmaceuticals, so I endeavored to find natural and sustainable alternatives. Each of us must do what works and feels best for us, but either way, I can provide a variety of suggestions for you to experiment with. Some of these tactics worked well for me personally and some worked well for other survivors I know.

The first step is one of the most commonly offered pieces of advice to anyone who has ever struggled with sleep issues: **Create a consistent bedtime routine.** I do not offer this suggestion to you lightly, because I am fully aware of the anxiety that this time of day can create for some of us. Bedtime can be one of the scariest of all times for trauma survivors, for a variety of reasons. Whether you struggle with recurring thoughts or fears playing on repeat in your mind, upsetting dreams, nightmares from your past, flashbacks, or the sheer terror of being faced with yourself in the dark and stuck in your own mind, nighttime can be one of the hardest times of the day, like a fever that rises in the wee hours.

If this is the case for you, and even if it's not, but you struggle to get the rest you need, creating a consistent bedtime routine full of activities and little extra touches that are soothing to you will be a great first step toward transforming your nighttime experience. The most important thing is to approach it with a sense of love and as a luxury that you can now afford to offer yourself.

What's involved in a bedtime routine? Whatever you want! But I'll give you some ideas to start with and you can experiment from there. To get started, determine what time you would need to get to sleep in order to get a full night's rest. The typical recommendation is anywhere from seven to nine hours, but you may need more. Philosophies vary widely on the optimal amount of sleep; however, I believe this to be a uniquely personal metric which varies, not only by individual, but also by a number of other fluctuating factors, such as activity level, age, gender, type of work, etc. In addition, this metric may fluctuate throughout the stages of recovery and life. How much sleep you require at any given point is something you will have to determine for yourself, and once you have, you can structure your bedtime routine accordingly.

I find that I operate at my best when I consistently have between eight and nine hours of sleep. In order to achieve this, my go-to-sleep-time goal is consistently eight and a half to nine hours before I know I need to be up the next day. To incorporate my full wind-down time, my *bedtime* is approximately sixty minutes before my go-to-sleep time. You may need more or less, depending on the wind-down routine you create.

The key to this routine is consistency. That means that, even on days when you don't necessarily need to get up at a certain time, you continue to maintain a similar bedtime. With only occasional exceptions, the best practice is not to exceed more than a thirty-minute fluctuation (earlier or later) in your go-to-sleep time. Just do your best. This will assist your mind and body in winding down and achieving more consistent and restful sleep over time. Ultimately, this is a gift that you are giving to yourself. Nervous system regulation thrives on routine and consistency.

Now for the fun part: Choose activities that you find to be soothing to incorporate into your wind down and bedtime routine. A hot bath including essential oils, candles and relaxing music is one friend's go-to relaxing activity. Since I have not had the luxury of a soaking tub at my disposal during my post-cult recovery period, I enjoyed hot showers at night with music that I love singing along to. Singing in a hot shower is just one step in my wind down routine that signals to my mind, heart and body that it is time to relax, let go, and settle into rest.

Incorporating aromatherapy and supplements are excellent options to explore as well. I have experimented with a range of naturally calming sleep aids, from CBD (cannabidiol) gummies to magnesium glycinate-based gummies, to various hot beverages, to sleep patches that gradually deliver melatonin, valerian and other rest-enhancing herbs into the body. Turning off unneeded lights and/or lighting candles is another nice touch to help create a relaxing atmosphere and trigger your mind and body to settle into rest. Choose candles with soothing, calming aromas for an added benefit. Or perhaps you might spritz your bedding with a calming lavender or chamomile linen spray.

I was not a regular hot tea drinker before I got out of the high control group. When I got out, however, I was recommended a tea to help with relieving anxiety and calming nerves which, when steeped at twice the recommended time, had a tremendously calming and sedating effect. I began to consume it religiously before bedtime and I could feel its effects significantly. Since then, I have become a regular nighttime tea drinker and have found that stress-relieving bedtime teas are another tool that assists me in winding down and signaling time for sleep. I've experimented with a variety of bedtime lattes and "sleepy time" teas with success. I recommend looking for herbal tea options that include kava root, ashwagandha, valerian root, chamomile, lavender, lemon balm, passionflower or any combination of these. In addition, tart cherry juice is known to support the body's natural melatonin production.

A quick internet search or visit to your local health foods store will yield a wide variety of healthy, natural calming aids and sleep supplements. Pick ones that appeal to you in a form that you find attractive. If you hate tea, for example, opt for a gummy, a skin-absorption patch or a capsule-based supplement instead.

Here's one of my favorite parts: Invest in bedding that you love and that will help to make you as comfortable as humanly possible at bedtime. This will make going to bed even more appealing and getting a good night's sleep even more likely. Multiple pillows, a fluffy comforter and luxuriously soft sheets are all essentials for me. This does not have to be a costly endeavor, either. All manner of bedding is available at affordable prices online or in discount stores, such as TJMaxx and HomeGoods (also known as TK Maxx, HomeSense, Winners and Marshalls, internationally).

Take your time to find the elements that feel comfortable, beautiful and luxurious to *you*. Putting conscious intention behind creating a welcoming and relaxing space for sleep is the key to success in this practice. It is a labor of love for *yourself*, fostering a sense of self-care, which is exactly what we want to cultivate in our life now. While recovery is hard work, so much of it is also about reclaiming softness, gentleness, kindness and love, especially toward ourselves.

Stepping away from electronic screens and devices an hour or two before bedtime may be another helpful tactic to incorporate into your wind-down time. While it has become increasingly difficult to disconnect from these tools in our modern society, you may experiment with this technique to see how it affects you over time. Some studies have shown that the absorption of blue light from these screens inhibits the body's natural process of melatonin production at night. Blue light aside, the stimulation from these devices can certainly run counter to the de-stimulation we crave for restful sleep.

Perhaps try replacing electronic-base activities with some reading material or a journaling habit prior to sleep instead. Maybe you create a skincare routine that helps you to feel nurtured and soothed. Maybe you do a short (or long!) writing session to unburden your mind of the thoughts and events of the day. Maybe some gentle music and stretching help to relax your muscles as well as your mind. Maybe a deep breathing session becomes a part of your wind-down ritual.

During sleeping hours, eliminating excess light is another critical component that positively contributes to sound, uninterrupted sleep. Light blocking curtains are essential in my bedroom. I even use an alarm clock with a display that automatically turns off during sleeping hours. As an even better bonus, it wakes me with a gradual sunrise-imitating light, culminating in gentle bird sounds, allowing me to emerge from sleep much more calmly and gently than the traditional blaring alarm I previously used. These little touches make bedtime and wake time more appealing, calming and conducive to a positive sleep experience.

You may also think about incorporating a white noise machine or playing gentle, soft music if you find silence deafening or threatening. On the other hand, if you require total silence, take whatever measures you need to eliminate noises, such as making sure you run appliances earlier in the day. Studies have shown that cool temperatures at night are more conducive to sound sleep, so keep that in mind in creating your nighttime environment, as well.

Not only do we spend around one-third of our life sleeping, but the quality of that time has an incredible impact on how we experience and feel during the waking hours of our life. Working toward achieving and maintaining quality rest will have long-lasting positive impacts on our nervous system regulation efforts. How we wake up and begin our day matters as well. You may be amazed at how a gentle form of morning alarm impacts your entire sleep game. Many alternatives to the traditional alarm clock now exist. You might like to use a watch with an alarm that gently vibrates to wake you up. You may opt for a sunrise alarm that wakes you with gradually increasing light and nature sounds or soft tunes. This system allows your body to gently rise from its sleep cycles in accordance with your natural circadian rhythm. These calmer, or more gradual waking tools can positively impact not only your rest time, but also, your state of mind upon waking.

I encourage you to approach this process with a sense of fun and adventure. It should be about fostering relaxation, treating yourself kindly and creating comfort in your day to day routine. Your routine can be as long or as short as you choose and you can expand or reduce it at any time based on what serves you best. Once you create a routine of activities and elements that you love, that calm you and that offer you a little bit of personal luxury, **and you consistently engage in this routine**, your mind and body will begin to automatically transition into this mode of relaxation as you prepare for rest. Over time, that relaxation can deepen more and more as you come to build positive associations with bedtime. This practice can gradually lead not only to deeper and more prolonged rest at night, but to increased relaxation throughout your waking hours as well. It can do wonders for resetting and calming your entire nervous system.

Being Good To Yourself

Relationships are work. We've all heard this and it's true. Relationships require time, attention and energy in order to nurture them and to see them thrive. This maxim is true not only of relationships with others, but also in regard to your *relationship with yourself.* Too often, we forget entirely that our relationship with ourselves even exists, much less that it requires our time, attention and energy.

The most important relationship you will ever have IS the relationship with yourself. It is the one relationship that remains with you in every moment of every day, with every breath, from the moment you are born right through to the moment that you leave this world. And yet, it is often the most overlooked of them all, taken for granted and put on the back burner. During long-term abusive and trauma-inducing situations, it is often the relationship that we lose touch with completely.

For survivors of narcissistic and cultic abuse, the loss of our sense of self was one of the first things to go in our previous lives. Regaining that sense of self is the foundation of our recovery. To a large degree, recovery from CPTSD is about reestablishing, and then re-building, our relationship with ourselves. Doing this work takes time and it is ongoing, so be patient with the process.

Most importantly, know that you are worth the effort, energy and attention that cultivating a relationship with yourself requires. Not only is a strong relationship with yourself the best possible protection from recurring abusive relationships, but it is also the greatest source of comfort and joy to which you will return for the rest of your days. The way that you treat yourself sets the standard for how you expect to be treated *by* others and what you will allow *from* others. Keep that in mind as you foster kindness, patience, gentleness and love toward yourself.

In the spirit of gently rebuilding this connection, I recommend putting conscious effort into doing something a little extra kind for yourself on a regular basis, whether daily, weekly or monthly, or better yet, all of the above! Find gifts to offer yourself that support this reconnection process and that you can also look forward to throughout your process. Make a point of finding time to work these into your day-to-day life wherever possible. What's important is that you treat them with the same level of priority as mandatory tasks like going to work, cleaning the house and all the other necessary minutiae of everyday survival.

These gifts may be, but don't need to be, physical items. Gifting yourself a block of time for stillness and reflection, a hot bath, reading a fun book or maybe taking a nap are all beautiful offerings to yourself. Self-care can include moments of luxury like a pedicure or a massage, but at the end of the day, self-care is truly about how we treat ourselves, speak to ourselves and the standards and boundaries we set for ourselves. Self-care is about *loving* ourselves and that, my friend, is an internal act, not an external action. Genuine self-care will be reflected in the choices we make for ourselves as a result of building, and investing in, that most important relationship of all: the relationship within.

Once I was out of the high-control group, had my own place and started to experience enough energy to do more than come home from work and veg out in front of the TV, I began to dabble in the kitchen again. Before the group completely took over every waking hour of my life and every waking thought in my mind, back when I was first discovering myself in my earliest years of life, I enjoyed a great love for cooking, and especially, baking. It was one of my first passions. Stepping back into the kitchen to make more than just a cursory meal was a luxury that I was excited to try out whenever I could muster the energy for it. I quickly rediscovered my love of baking (and of baked goods!), and in the process, I felt like I found a long-lost piece of myself that I'd so dearly missed. That piece of me was gone for so long, I wasn't aware of how deeply I missed it until I reconnected with it.

There are so many discoveries to be made in these first years out. Expressing myself through "kitchen crafts," as I like to call it, became a great outlet for my creativity, but also for self-nurturing. At the same time, I got to share these gifts with others, who, I discovered, were just as thrilled and delighted to take part in my kitchen crafts as I was to share them. Such a seemingly simple, unremarkable act was actually a catalyst for deep healing.

I also got to rediscover my love of reading for pleasure. This was a luxury which I was not afforded in the previous decade. Unfortunately, now that I was free, I discovered that my capacity for the focus and attention span required to read was greatly diminished. I learned that this diminished capacity is a common side effect experienced from years of coercive control (also known as mind control), but it was very frustrating all the same. Nonetheless, I began to indulge in short bursts of recreational reading on a regular basis, several times a week. I would make a point of reading a couple of pages of a novel at bedtime when I could keep my eyes open. Gradually, over a longer period than I would have liked, my capacity began to increase for greater amounts of reading time. The important thing is that it *did* increase.

Reconnecting with the things that are quintessentially *you,* and/or discovering the things that are *now* you, is not only an extremely necessary part of the recovery process, but it can be an extremely pleasurable one as well! You might make a list of things that come to mind and add to it as new memories or ideas surface. You don't have to do it all at once. Just pick the top one or two things that interest you and begin to play with them when you have the energy. You will need to be conscious about creating the time and space for it. This may be one of your gifts to yourself.

The things that I gradually found time for which brought me back to myself were: reading; writing; baking; cooking; crocheting; going to the movies; sleeping in on the weekends; spending mornings off "lazily" relaxing in my pajamas with a cup of coffee, staring out the window and thinking; journaling; "gardening" with a handful of small, potted plants in my tiny studio apartment; kickboxing; dancing and singing in my living room; venturing out to try new coffee shops and bakeries by myself; hiking in the woods; and taking exploratory day trips to places I'd never been. Make your own list, take your time and have fun rediscovering—and rebuilding—a safe and beautiful world full of positive experiences.

In addition to these larger scale activities, begin incorporating healthy, nurturing acts of kindness for you and your body into your daily, weekly or monthly plans. The key to successfully reconnecting with yourself through these activities is to do them with conscious, loving intention and to be present with yourself throughout them. These are relatively simple acts of love that you can easily incorporate, such as:

- Engaging in a deep relaxation exercise
- Thoughtfully cooking yourself (or taking yourself out for) a nourishing meal
- Having a long soak in a hot bath
- Adding a calming supplement or vitamins to your daily routine
- Going for a walk in nature
- Dancing and singing with abandon
- Sitting quietly with a hot cup of tea (or beverage of choice) and spending a few moments enjoying deep breaths
- Getting a massage
- Giving yourself a foot massage
- Spending ten minutes gently stretching your muscles from head to toe
- Spending five minutes practicing a grounding exercise (see Chapter 7: Go Natural, for one example)
- Speaking kind and encouraging words to yourself when you see your reflection in a mirror.

Coming from my cultic group where bodies were disregarded and where I was perpetually dissociating, it took time to shift my focus toward seeing, hearing and feeling my body. I am continually repairing and deepening this connection. It is important, because reconnecting with our bodies naturally assists us in reconnecting with our inner self. Taking care of the physical body and our physical needs is one of the most fundamental aspects of this process, because until our most basic, primal needs are met, it is nigh impossible to move beyond survival mode. Reconstructing a stable world and safe reality around us is foundational to moving toward deeper healing. Once those basic needs are met, we can find more energy, focus and means to meet our deeper needs.

For many of us, these basic needs will involve finding a safe place to live, setting up our homes, finding employment and securing a stable income, and creating a routine for accomplishing necessary everyday tasks. This is the ground level of meeting our core needs. Until we have successfully mastered this level of survival, most of our physical and mental energetic resources will need to go toward these matters.

As we begin to find our footing in a new, safe world, we can begin to allow ourselves to face the scarier issues beneath the surface. There is no set timeline for this process, however. It will vary greatly from person to person. There are a multitude of factors that determine each individual's progress down this path, which is why there is absolutely NO way to judge or measure ourselves against anyone else doing this work. We are all healing from our own unique traumas and we will all do it in our own, unique way and our own, unique timing specific to our personal needs, pasts, desires and healthy rate of growth. Remember the spiral of healing. You will be offered infinite opportunities to revisit your emotional, spiritual, mental and physical healing needs from new levels as you go along.

Now that we've conquered some of the physical needs and methods of reconnection, let's take a deeper look at how we can begin to address our mental and emotional needs.

A Gentle Reminder

Our bodies *want* to heal. I find this concept to be incredibly comforting and encouraging. The natural intelligence of the body organically tends toward healing, and given the proper support, it will do so. We don't have to fight against it to force it into "shape" or good health. Instead, we need to work *with* it.

I believe that our minds work similarly. When the proper conditions and ingredients are presented to move toward calm and balance, our minds naturally tend toward healing with a shift to uplifting and supportive internal dialogue. This is great news! It means that our bodies and minds will work *with* us in all our efforts to bring these aspects back into health and balance. We do not have to fight to gain control over them; rather, we can adopt a mindset of collaboration with our bodies and minds as we re-build our internal communication system. This allows our body and mind's natural tendencies to propel us toward greater health, even when we are not consciously "working" at it.

Healing is a process and much of it is simply about providing the proper soil in which this healing can take place. We cannot commit ourselves to active, conscious healing work twenty-four hours a day, seven days a week. Nor should we. We delve into these practices as we are able to hold space for them, and then we step away and trust the process to continue behind the scenes while we carry on with our lives. It is equally important that we remember to go out into the world, live our lives and ***enjoy*** **life right here and now**, in the present. Just like any job, it is not healthy to work 24/7. Allow yourself breaks, both physical *and* mental. Trust the process and know that it is an *ongoing* process, not a final destination. Remember to enjoy your journey! After all, isn't that the whole point? We must remind ourselves to stop waiting for "one day" and to enjoy ourselves *today*. This *is* the time that you have been waiting for.

5

The Importance of Talking to Yourself

In trauma, not only did we commonly dissociate from our bodies, but we find our minds and hearts have become fractured and disconnected as well. For those recovering from cultic or narcissistic abuse, making simple decisions such as what to eat and what to wear might feel overwhelming, let alone larger tasks like setting up a new home or making employment decisions. We have been so severed from the most basic self-knowledge—knowing our own minds and our own hearts—due to the usurping of that role by external forces. Often, we have had our decisions dictated to us, choices taken away entirely, or been told so often and in so many ways that we don't know *how* to make those (good) choices that we have come to entirely lose touch with the simple, innate ability to know our own mind. So much mental and emotional abuse can leave survivors feeling hopelessly confused, uncertain and stripped of their natural confidence. Reconnecting with our true self is like catching up with an old friend from childhood and learning about who they are now.

During my time in the therapy group, the leader would commonly accuse me (and others) of being indecisive. He had the final say in any decision, no matter how large or trivial, because we (women, in particular) were so indecisive, he claimed. The truth is that I was not indecisive at all. In many cases, I knew exactly what I wanted, thought, or preferred. However, I learned from our interactions over many years that my preferences and desires were secondary to his and that his decisions would *always* win out over anyone else's. It didn't take long for me to give up on expressing myself and to defer to his decisions and desires, just as all those around him did. Much like in the family dynamic where I was raised, I was carefully groomed to cede my own mind to my leader's and he simply used the accusation of "indecisiveness" to justify it.

In the life after, I have learned that it is less about not knowing my mind and more about believing in my worth. I was never indecisive. I just didn't know, or believe, that I deserved to be heard, to be listened to and to have the things I wanted. I chose to forego these rights for the *safety* provided by giving the leader what he wanted. For many of us, this tactic is absolutely necessary as we navigate and live within the systems of high control situations. In recovery, however, I have learned that determining my own mind is not the greatest challenge. No; the greatest challenge is learning that I deserve to have a say, to have my needs met, my wants heard and my preferences respected.

It may take time to remember who you were before the trauma and decide who you want to be now. For those who were born and raised in these circumstances, there may be no "before" time to reconnect with, but you can still discover who you are *now*. With the right mindset, this can be an incredibly enjoyable and satisfying endeavor. One of the first steps you might take along this journey is simply talking to yourself. In what form you choose to talk to yourself will be individual to you. All that matters is that you rebuild your internal communication system.

For some, this may involve having conversations with yourself out loud in the privacy of your own home or other private space. It may be sitting still, quietly, and allowing yourself to think through all the thoughts and ideas swirling in your head. For me, it is often a hybrid of these two things, in which I mull over some thoughts and then find myself responding to them out loud.

Any form of writing or journaling that appeals to you is another excellent way to rebuild that internal communication system. You may choose to do stream of consciousness writing, which is an excellent way to get all the swirling thoughts out of your head and outside of you so that you can find the deeper feelings, thoughts and answers below them. Stream of consciousness writing requires nothing more than suspending total judgment and writing down literally every single thing that passes through your mind, from "I really need to do laundry", to " I have a weird pain in my right side", to "I really don't want to do this, I have nothing to say", to "I'm so angry I was robbed of my dignity", and so on and so forth. The key to this style of writing is to keep the pen moving. You just keeping writing whatever is in your head, even if you feel like you've gone blank. I have written "I have nothing to say" or "my head is blank" over and over again until something else surfaced. Usually I find that this is a panic response to the rule to keep the pen (or keyboard) moving, and by simply honoring it by writing it down repeatedly, I begin to relax and new material will soon follow. As you continue to write, the surface level thoughts get cleared away and deeper thoughts are finally given voice. This process can lead to a great deal of discovery, clarity and relief.

For others, the writing could take another form, such as making lists or even writing haikus! I know a trauma survivor who became known for her prolific haikus. The structure of the haikus can provide a structure to focus on, serving to bring one into the moment and transforming that moment into a creative act.

Still others may find that a different creative act provides that same level of insight and clarity. Drawing, painting and writing music are a handful of other ways that may provide an avenue for internal communication building. Creative acts in general help us to reconnect with our inner selves because they come from a deeply personal place and they are always unique to the individual.

For some, singing can be an incredible outlet for verbalizing your thoughts and feelings. Singing used in this way can be an amazing blend of both somatic and internal healing. If using singing, however, it's important to allow yourself to express your own thoughts and feelings through the act of singing.

The point is, once again, to reconnect with your own mind and to allow yourself to feel your feelings. Talking to ourselves is another way in which we can do this. Despite its unbelievable simplicity, this can be such a scary task that it is super common to avoid it. In fact, that's pretty much what we're taught to do in this world. You don't have to be recovering from trauma to be afraid to genuinely feel your feelings. Avoidance of this very thing generally sits at the root of any kind of addiction.

In the first six months after I got out, I would swing back and forth between reveling in the freedom to sit quietly and consider my own thoughts and numbing out completely with movies and television. I honestly believe both were helpful, and allowing myself to be where I was within the process was just as important to my healing as anything else. As we gradually begin to reconnect with our own minds, the easier it becomes and the less intimidating. Over time, once I began to know my own mind again, it became a source of comfort and safety in which I craved to spend time and take solace when I went too long neglecting it. To love ourselves, we must know ourselves.

If you will suspend judgment of yourself, as mentioned in the beginning, then you will most likely experience some relief, simply from the act of letting your thoughts and feelings have a voice. One of the truly magical aspects of using writing as a tool for this practice is the innate ability for that act to give us perspective and sometimes transform our entire understanding or interpretation of a situation in our lives. It's not about being a great writer. It's simply about giving your internal voice an outlet and allowing your own wise, internal guidance system an opportunity to navigate the situation objectively. The relief I experience from this practice is priceless.

Regardless of your preferred method for building that internal communication, it is so very important that you take great care with how you respond to the messages and information you receive during this process. Suspending your self-judgment is the first step. The second step is responding to yourself with love, grace and support, just as if your dearest friend were pouring out her heart to you. We must become our own dearest friends, and that means, we must listen to our minds and hearts with compassion and empathy. Yes, this means that you must feel and allow yourself to express emotions of all kinds. It also means that you must respond appropriately to the information you receive by providing yourself with the support and fulfillment of whatever needs are exposed, to the best of your ability.

The many different forms of self-care that we are covering in this book will likely be one of the forms of fulfillment your inner self will require, whether it is a physical need, an emotional need or a spiritual need. When we respond to the messages and information that we uncover through this internal communication system by showing support, compassion and nurturance, we honor it and teach ourselves that it is not only safe to express our innermost thoughts and feelings, but that we now have the *power* to move accordingly. As such, it becomes easier, faster and smoother to know our own hearts and minds and to act on that knowing. This consequence results in greater self-confidence, greater clarity, and instills safeguards to protect us from falling prey to further abusers or abusive situations. It is a win-win for every part of our body, mind, heart and soul.

6

Quiet the Mind, Open the Heart

Okay, it's time to get down and dirty on planning how exactly you are going to begin to put this self-care thing into serious practice. It won't happen on its own. It takes conscious effort, and that is why it is considered work, even though it results in some serious relaxation and a multitude of mental, physical and emotional benefits. In reality, however, this is the fun part! This is where you get to figure out exactly what works for you and begin to add it into your everyday life. This is where *life* starts to get *good.*

You deserve this.

Only YOU can do this for you.

And **you are worth it**.

Now, let's get to it.

Creating Comfort

It's time to start creating comfort, not just within yourself, as in the internal haven we have been creating in our own minds and hearts, but also in your external world. There are endless ways to do that, and each person will be attracted to different things. Discovering what those things are for you, and incorporating them into your world, can be a fun adventure.

On the other hand, perhaps you already know! Even better. Then it's time to take what you know and start building on it. This is *your* life now. You get to choose what it looks, feels, smells, tastes and sounds like.

For me, rebuilding my life in these early years of recovery has been a gradual process. When I escaped my culty life, I had very little left. I had to start over and rebuild my physical world, mostly from scratch. While that was daunting at first, it became a part of my recovery process. I had to ask myself, and decide, what I wanted now, what I liked now, who I *was* now. Some of it was familiar and some of it was new to me.

One thing I have always highly valued is softness in textures. Pillows, blankets, clothes, etc. I crave softness in my life. For me, it was essential to create surroundings that were full of softness, since that equates to comfort in my mind. I encourage you to try adding some softness wherever you can. Find a super-soft blanket and throw pillow that you can wrap yourself in at the end of a long day and rest your head on. Buy a super-soft pair of lounge pants that you can wear around your home.

Softness isn't only tactile. Maybe try introducing some soft lighting into your living space to create a soothing ambiance. Play some gentle music that you enjoy. I am a fan of all kinds of music, but there is something sublime about gentle music playing with some beautifully scented candles lit, while cushioned or wrapped in soft textures. It may be instrumental music, meditation music, nature sounds, classical music, lo-fi tunes or just some low-key lyrical melodies. Whatever moves you or appeals to you.

Keep a small "something sweet" on hand. When I first got out, a friend told me that it was important to eat something sweet after talking about, or dealing with, trauma. It is symbolic. The idea is that sweetness is needed to counter the bitterness and restore balance. I find that sweetness and softness are the two aspects my life needed so much more of as I entered recovery. I like to keep a little candy dish on hand with bite-size pieces of sweetness. I think it's important to give ourselves that sweetness free of any guilt or self-judgment (which would sabotage the entire purpose). See if this works for you or find your own version of sweetness that you can offer yourself when needed to counter the bitterness of trauma in your recovery work.

While all this sounds perfectly decadent—and to many of us it is—there is more to it than simple luxury. For those recovering from trauma, the dissociation that we developed often prevents us from truly being in the moment and experiencing life. Staying present while giving yourself positive, physical experiences will help to retrain your mind and body to the awareness that they are safe to live together once again. The key is to be present with these experiences of physical delight. Not only do you deserve it, but they are helping to heal you.

Dissociation aside, every single one of us who is recovering from trauma is working to calm and regulate our *compromised* (to put it delicately) nervous systems. Creating comfort in your world is not *only* an act of love for yourself and it is definitely not *just* some silly indulgence. It is a practice of physical repair for your nervous system. This is just one of the super important reasons for you to do this "work" of creating comfort in your life and your environment.

Imagine coming home at the end of a long day, slipping into the softest, coziest pair of lounge pants, lighting some lovely candles, turning on some gentle music and curling up into a pile of pillows. How does your nervous system feel just *thinking* of that scenario? And how much more attractive does the work of being still and listening to yourself become?

And if that's *not* what does it for you, let's figure out what does! Maybe it's going for a leisurely walk in nature or cuddling with a furry best friend. Spend some serious time thinking about it, maybe do some free writing about it, start looking around and noticing what calls to you and/or talk to others about what makes their heart sing. If you don't already know what feels luxurious to you, this can be a truly fun period of research as you get to discover these new parts of yourself.

Listen, you have survived your own personal hell. It is time to take that badass accomplishment and make it worthwhile. There's a good chance that no one else will have any clue how hard the survival and recovery process you're going through actually is, so it is up to *you* to acknowledge it for yourself and do what you can to create some ease and comfort in this process for yourself. Your time has come. Make it count, and wherever possible, make it fun.

Meditation Practices

> ***Disclaimer:*** *For those who are recovering from certain circles of spiritual, religious, self-help and/or therapy-based abusive situations where meditation practices were used in harmful and controlling ways, the following section may not be for you. As I mentioned in the beginning, I discovered in my first days out of the group that some mindfulness exercises increased my anxiety and were therefore counterproductive for me. If meditation-based healing modalities are triggering and/or problematic for you, please do not push yourself to pursue them. As always, take what works for you and leave what does not.*

Just before heading to bed at night, I enjoy performing some deep muscle-release stretches while following a short, guided meditation. I also like to start my mornings with this practice. It bookends my day with an experience of deep relaxation and self-care, setting the tone for both the day, and the night, to come.

Meditation has become widely acknowledged in scientific and medical circles for its health benefits. Quieting the mind and slowing down our internal worlds is not only beneficial to the body, it creates some much-needed space in our hearts and minds for peace, calm and clarity. However, there are many forms and practices for meditation, and which one sits best with you may take some experimentation. Regardless of the form, it will almost certainly require practice.

Meditation practices serve to invite more mindfulness into our day-to-day activities and assist in regulating the nervous system. This mindfulness can be particularly helpful for those of us working our way back to the land of the living through the recovery process. Since the recovery effort truly is a process, and one in which we are most likely to engage to some degree for the rest of our lives, ongoing tools like meditation become essential to everyday life. The space that mindfulness gradually creates in our inner worlds can help us see, cope with, and even rise above the trauma triggers which may sometimes seem to rule our lives.

For some, meditation may be considered a spiritual practice, but it doesn't have to be. It can also be simply a form of self-care. And on top of that, there are SO many ways to meditate. It's not only sitting in a cross-legged position, eyes closed, thumb and middle finger resting together on your knees. Sure, that's one way to do it, but that's far from the *only* way to do it.

You can meditate while you're walking, meditate while you're washing dishes, meditate while you're taking a shower, meditate while you're feeding the dog. You can meditate via a guided soundtrack or through prescribed breathing exercises. You can meditate while painting or singing or staring at the ceiling.

To me, meditation is just another form of practice in learning to recognize, hear and listen to my own inner voice, my intuition, the inherent guidance system within all of us. As we discussed in Chapter 2, tuning into that radio station is so important to finding sure footing in our new worlds and avoiding the pitfalls that lead us into unhealthy situations, environments and relationships. In addition, it is an excellent tool for calming and regulating the nervous system. The more we are able to regulate our nervous systems in our general day to day, the faster it can heal and the more adept we become at regulating it when we are triggered and upset.

One of the benefits of guided meditations for the C-PTSD "monkey mind" is that it can help us to stay focused during the meditation time. I also like that I can choose from a vast variety of topics in my guided meditation, from general positive vibes, to cultivating self-love, to bringing in inner calm and clarity—there's truly something for everything. There are other times, however, when I just want to sit still and allow my inner thoughts and feelings to flow so that I can work out a concern or an issue in my life. In these times, I like to also create the conditions that will help me to calm myself and be still. I might play some meditative music, light a candle, and get into a comfortable position where I can fully relax without falling asleep. Then I begin my process of focusing on my breathing, checking in with my body and asking my mind, what's up? This is a beautiful form of self-communication and self-care, and thanks to some practice and patience, I now know I can absolutely turn to this tool to get some clarity, calm, release or relief. You can too!

The ritual of turning on the music, lighting the candle and finding a comfy spot to relax, after some time, become early cues to my mind, heart and body about the mode that I am shifting into. Just like creating a wind down routine, simple rituals like this can cue your inner and outer worlds, helping you to relax into this space faster and easier over time. You can weave these simple routines into any part of your day, to anchor in a moment of peace or grounding.

If you'd like to try out some guided meditation or some chill, meditative music to create your own calming ritual, but you don't know where to start, I recommend turning to a music streaming platform such as Spotify, iTunes, or YouTube. There's a vast array of music and meditation options to choose from. You can search whatever appeals to you. You might try "Calming mediation music," "Guided meditation for self-love," "guided meditation for relaxation," "guided meditation for calming nervous system," "meditation sounds," "calming music," or whatever vibe you're feeling in the moment.

There are so many channels that create these materials and are free to access. One of my favorite guided meditation channels is called "Great Meditations" on YouTube; it has an extensive catalog of approachable guided meditation videos with no commercial interruptions. They range anywhere from 5 to 60 minutes long.

The greatest hurdle we face in accomplishing these simple tasks of self-care is usually just the act of getting started. Stopping what we are doing to start a ten-minute meditation feels annoying, disruptive, impractical, or simply not appealing as we stay absorbed in our other all-consuming activities. Even though I absolutely love the way I feel while I'm in the midst of one of these meditations, it is still sometimes a struggle to talk myself into stopping everything else in order to do it (or delaying sleep by ten minutes in order to fit it in). I've never once regretted doing it after the fact, but it can take some willpower to get started, even after it becomes a routine. Don't underestimate this challenge. This is why healing is *work* even when it's something that we want more than anything else. Be good to yourself by being your own gentle parent and insisting that you consume the self-care routines that you have found work for you, like insisting that your inner child eats her broccoli *with* her mac 'n cheese.

If you prefer to spend some quiet time relaxing without any guided imagery or assistance, that is awesome too. All that matters is that you explore and find what works best for you. Have fun experimenting, researching, or practicing different techniques. And if you want to try it right now, all you need to do is put this book down, get into a comfortable position—*any* position that you find comfortable or relaxing—gently close your eyes and begin to pay attention to your breath. Notice whether you are holding your breath or how you are breathing. Usually, just the simple act of noticing will cause you to shift your breathing in some way. You may breathe more deeply or more steadily. It doesn't really matter at this stage. Right now, you are just noticing. If noticing causes you to crave a deeper breath or slower breath, then honor that. There is no right or wrong.

As you allow yourself to breathe freely and you focus on your breath, give your body permission to relax. You can perform a simple internal scan of your body, starting at the top of your head and gradually working your way all the way down to your toes. Notice all the places you are holding tension, from the top of your head to your face, to your jaw, to your neck, down to your shoulders and arms, down your back, through your hips, butt, thighs, knees, calves and ankles. As you slowly scan, allow your muscles to relax as much as possible at each point and then keep going. Once you've made it all the way down to your toes, come back to your breath. How has it changed? How do you feel now, in your mind and in your body? What thoughts or feelings are wanting your attention now, if any?

Congratulations! You just completed a simple, calming, self-care meditation exercise. Take note of how you felt before, during and after it. Notice whether you have an aversion to doing it again or can't wait to do it again. Whatever you discover in this practice, it is information. Once again, there is no right or wrong. This is just part of the journey of uncovering and discovering what works for you as you commit yourself further to your own healing and recovery process.

Take note: *If a particular self-care practice or technique does* *or does not work for you right now, that is totally okay. Just remember that it doesn't mean that it will or will not work for you in the future. As we evolve, grow and heal, so do our needs and our desires. This is a journey of continual discovery that requires us to stretch our willingness to change. Be willing to reconsider, return to, and re-experiment with options that previously did not suit you, as well as to release and move on from options that no longer serve you.*

If you have made it this far, I am super proud of you! *Seriously.* Some might scoff or drastically underestimate the value and importance of taking a few minutes to do such a simple exercise. I cannot. I am all too familiar with the metaphorical demons that lie hidden in our subconscious minds that will do anything to deter us from taking these steps. I know how incredible a feat it is to take even five minutes to sit still with yourself and feel what lies within. I know the terror that can prevent a person from *ever* taking such courageous steps. But that is not you. You are one of the warriors who has chosen to take your destiny into your own hands and face the darkness that would keep you imprisoned. This is hero's work and there is no set timetable. It is not about how long it takes or how far you're able to go in a single sitting. It is *only* about your choice to keep going, at any pace at all.

Back to Breath

Let's take a brief moment to revisit block breathing. This is the technique we discussed in Chapter One, in which you count through your breaths.

Block breathing can, in and of itself, be used as a form of meditation.

You can do it with eyes open or closed. Start by inhaling on a four count, holding your breath for a count of four, exhaling on a four count and pausing. Do this a few times, counting in your mind for each stage. This exercise helps to bring us into the present moment and can pause spiraling thoughts and emotions. If you can employ this technique early enough, it can even help to prevent full blown panic attacks. Block breathing is simple enough to be done anywhere and any time, discreetly enough that no one even notices.

Also, remember the powerful effect of conscious breathing in which you make your exhales double the length of your inhales? This is an excellent technique for releasing built up, pent up, anxious or stressful energy. After any fight, flight, freeze or fawn moment, try doubling your exhales to rapidly release the fearful energy and bring your parasympathetic nervous system back online to stabilize and regulate you. It can also be beneficial to add an audible sigh to your exhale or to blow the air out through your lips, allowing them to vibrate that energy out of your body. However you do it, the most important part is that your exhales extend beyond your inhales: Inhale on a four count and exhale on an eight count. I have practiced this technique in a variety of ways and I feel the calming benefits with every version. See for yourself which way gives you the most ooey-gooey relaxation goodness.

A Word About Routines and Gratitude

Creating routines and daily rituals is one of the ways to restore a sense of balance and to create calm and peace in your everyday life. One of my greatest struggles resulting from living in ongoing trauma-inducing situations has been the perpetual and fundamental feeling of being unsafe and insecure. A lack of stability, normalcy and sense of solid ground creates undue strain on daily life. Especially if we have grown up in unpredictable, chaotic and/or unsafe environments, we are likely to carry this sense of insecurity into our adult lives.

Routines and rituals help to create some stability and normalcy. They give our lives the structure with which we can begin to build a sense of safety and security around the little part of the world that is within our direct control. Much of this book is about ways to build your own sense of solid foundation by establishing a loving structure around your life through healthy routines, such as your nighttime wind down routine. Creating routines is yet another place where you get to explore and discover what you love and what works for you.

For example, a morning cup of coffee can be an important, grounding ritual in your daily life. Pair this cup with a few moments of quiet with yourself. Maybe create a ritual of reflecting on, and writing down, three things you are grateful for as you drink your morning beverage. They could be simple expressions (e.g.: I am so grateful for this hot cup of coffee that I get to drink this morning) or they can be profound (e.g.: I am so grateful to finally be free). It's not about the specific content so much as it is about genuinely *feeling* the gratitude in your heart and body. This practice is literally training your mind to seek out and hone in on the bright spots in life—a daunting task when your mind and nervous system have been overwhelmed by stress and darkness for long periods of time. The more you do this, however, the easier it becomes and the more pleasant moments your mind finds to focus on. Finding even the smallest things to be grateful for can plant seeds of light in your heart that, when watered, *will* blossom into some seriously beautiful feelings of joy.

7

Nature and Nutrition: Regaining Health From the Outside In

A holistic approach to recovery must include both inner and outer aspects of healing from harnessing the resources that live both within us and in the world around us. As dynamic beings, I believe that a multifaceted approach is necessary to rebuild the connections between these inner and outer worlds. Let's discuss some of the tools and key components that I have found to be essential in regaining health on all levels.

Spending Time in Nature

Spending time in nature has been one of the most healing steps I have taken since I escaped the daily trauma of cult life. At first, I didn't have energy to go out on hikes or exploratory adventures. The best I could manage was sitting on a porch and watching the birds come and go. That, alone, was beneficial.

As time went on, after many months of recovery had passed, I found enough energy to go walking on some simple nature trails. As I discovered the new city in which I lived, and the surrounding areas, I made it a priority to find easy hikes where I could spend time outdoors surrounded by nature. The effect was transformative.

I believe that spending time in nature—and in particular, spending time alone in nature—is one of the most impactful steps that we can take in our healing and recovery journeys. There are so many ways to accomplish this, depending on where you live and what resources are available to you. In some cases, you may have to get creative to find ways to receive the benefits of connecting with yourself in nature.

There are many proven health benefits from spending time outside in nature. Just *looking* at trees, or the ocean, has been shown to lower heart rates and reduce tension in the body. Breathing in fresh air and moving your body outdoors has myriad healthful impacts on our being, not just physically, but mentally, emotionally and even spiritually.

I strongly encourage you to make it a priority to spend time connecting with yourself in a little piece of nature. This may mean simply sitting in a park under a tree. If you have access to a body of water—a river, lake, pond, stream or the ocean—then you have an incredible advantage. Just being near a body of water affords opportunity to invite its calming and healing energy into your space, whether by walking near it, sitting by it, or actually submersing part of yourself in the water. I find that just sitting by a swimming pool is incredibly calming.

Spending a few minutes in the sunshine, allowing the sun's rays to warm and penetrate your skin, enables your body to begin the natural Vitamin D synthesis process. It is quite literally bringing health to our bodies on both micro and macro levels. These processes naturally serve to boost our mood and emotional well-being.

Go for a hike through the woods, climb a mountain, swim in a lake, dive into waves at the beach, sit on the ground in a park and run your fingers through the grass, walk barefoot in the dirt or in the sand or on a patch of grass, find a nature trail near you and go for a bike ride, or simply take a walk through your neighborhood. Take advantage of *whatever* natural attributes you have available to you, *whenever* you can. Put away or turn off electronic devices and allow yourself to just be present in that space. This is a great time to focus on your breath and allow yourself to enjoy some deep inhales, oxygenating your blood, invigorating your body and clearing your mind. If you give yourself the space and time to be completely present with yourself out in nature, you may be surprised by what you uncover.

The experience of truly being with myself in these natural environments is quite different from sitting with myself at home on the couch. Both have value, but there is something inherently cleansing and rejuvenating about this time spent outdoors. I urge you to give yourself this experience, in whatever environment or capacity best suits you.

The best part is that you really don't need anything special to engage in this tremendously healing and helpful practice. It doesn't cost anything either. It is one of the most abundant and easily accessible resources that you can tap into whenever you choose.

Worst case scenario, if you cannot physically put yourself in a natural environment for one reason or another, there is always the internet! YouTube is full of spectacular videos of every type of natural environment. You can find all manner of nature videos full of landscapes, underwater-scapes, and all sorts of wildlife. If no other option is available, allow yourself to spend time absorbing the energy of nature vicariously through these videos. It is certainly not the same as being physically present in nature yourself. However, you can still receive a number of the healthful benefits in your body through this virtual sensory stimulation.

The Healing Power of Nature
A Grounding and Emotional Clearing Exercise

Here is an exercise to experiment with next time you are outdoors* with a few minutes to indulge in some vital self-care. This exercise can be done as quickly or as slowly as you like, so time constraints need not be a deterrent.

Find a comfortable place to sit or lie down. If you can sit directly on the earth itself, that's even better. Turn your attention to your breath with the goal of noticing it. Then, take a couple of comfortably deep, slow breaths and feel your shoulder muscles loosen. If it's comfortable and safe to do so, you may gently close your eyes.

Feel the ground or structure beneath you, supporting you. Be present with that physical point of connection. Spread your palms flat and gently press them into the surface supporting you. Breathe.

Imagine that the base of your spine transforms into roots that are extending deep into the ground beneath you. See the roots growing and expanding, through the surface of the earth, down through the layers of dirt and sand, past other roots, past layers of sediment, then rock, through rivers of water deep in the earth's body, down and down all the way until they reach the earth's molten, lava core.

Now imagine that all the anxiety, tension, worry, stress, fear, negativity and preoccupations of your mind and body are draining away through these roots, all the way down to the core of the earth. Allow this energy to drain away through the roots as you feel your body relax. You may notice a sense of calm, easier breath, or a sense of more "space" within your body or mind. Whatever you experience, just take note of it. There is no right or wrong sensation.

Once this energy has traveled down to that molten, lava core, it is transmuted into pure, neutral energy. Be thankful for this safe place to deposit the old, unneeded energy.

Now draw your attention back up through the layers of the earth and begin to take note of the sensations of nature around you. Feel the sun beating down on your head, the air wrapping itself around your skin, any sounds of nature that surround you, any smells, etc. Come back to your breath and breathe in deeply. Invite the healing rays of the sun and the cleansing power of the wind and air to fill your body and whole being with fresh, clear, vibrant energy. Imagine this positive, clean energy funneling down through the crown of your head and allow it to melt through your entire body, filling the space where the old, stuck, negative energy previously lived. Enjoy deep relaxing breaths as you invite the energy to fill your entire being and wrap around you like a warm, soft blanket sealing in all this goodness.

Stay here and enjoy the sensations for as long as you like. When you emerge, remember that you get to take this fresh, clean slate with you and that you can return to this healing power of the earth anytime you like. We are endlessly connected to the grounding energy of this earth.

**Note: While performing this exercise outdoors adds the extra benefits of* *direct contact with nature, this exercise can just as easily be done indoors with the same grounding and clearing benefits.*

The Healing Power of Animals

Spending time with or around animals can also yield profoundly calming and healing benefits, similar to those of spending time outdoors. One of the magical aspects of getting out in nature, I find, is the proximity it creates between me and wildlife. When I'm hiking along a trail in the woods and suddenly, out of nowhere, a deer jumps across the path ahead of me and trots off to meet up with another deer further into the woods, time stands still for a moment and the atmosphere is electrified.

Or perhaps I glimpse a small movement out of the corner of my eye and I turn to see a little chipmunk perched on a fallen branch among the leaves, frozen in motion, warily observing me. I freeze too, and observe him right back. After these shared moments, I continue on, basking in the symphony of sounds echoing above my head as birdsong fills the air.

These little encounters help to bring me *fully* into the moment...if I let them. I urge you to allow yourself to be enchanted by all the life that is being lived out in nature. Allow yourself to absorb these experiences, to be fully present with them, and to receive the little offerings of health that they provide, physically, mentally and emotionally. Allow yourself to be a *part* of the life surrounding you, just another one of the animals out in the wild that day. We share this space with them. When I am feeling utterly alone, I can find a sense of belonging out in nature, if nowhere else. Nature is rife with lessons to teach us about living and being in the world when we take the time to observe and learn from it.

Pets are another amazing way to connect with nature. We'll delve more into this later. If you don't have pets at home, there are still a number of ways you can spend up close and personal time with animals. Find your local animal shelter and pay them a visit. Even if you're unable to take an animal home, spending time with them at the shelter can not only offer great benefit to you but also to the animals who are residing there. You may even choose to volunteer time to help at the shelter or to foster animals in need.

Cat cafes are a phenomenon that have made their way to the US and have become increasingly popular. These offer another opportunity to spend some time up close and personal with animals. See if there is a cat cafe near you and stop in for a beverage and some cuddles with the furry friends there when you're needing a little extra emotional support.

Nutrition for Mind, Body and Soul

Overall, health comes from feeding ourselves nutrient-dense ingredients on all levels. This holds true for what we feed ourselves mentally and emotionally as well as physically. For optimal health, we need to find ways to feed our mind, spirit, heart and body the appropriate, nutrient-dense ingredients they require.

We've discussed many of the needed ways that we can learn to love and take care of ourselves mentally, emotionally and physically. We've looked at practices, exercises, routines and environment. Let's also take a moment to spotlight the importance of what we put *in* our minds, hearts and bodies. What does a daily diet of self-love look like?

The Importance of Physical Nutrition

This is a biggie. It's no secret that what we put in our body affects how our body feels. However, juggling food and nutrition can be a full-time job. Just learning to decode fact from fiction in the world of nutrition, not to mention dodging all the personal agendas of the myriad exercise and health "gurus" out there, requires research scientist and ninja skills combined!

I have become so overwhelmed by navigating this crazy world in our western culture on so many different occasions that I finally had to nail down my own, fool-proof approach. The basis of it is: "Simple is beautiful." And in the spirit of that idea, I will share some recommendations on how to navigate this area for yourself.

Let me start by saying: *I love food.* I don't just love to eat, I love all things food. I love making it, I love exploring and experimenting with it, I love the aspect of community that it encourages, and I love the comfort that it provides. Of all things, food is intensely primal. Food is personal. Food is emotional. Food, like air and water, is essential to life.

For that reason, I will not tell you what to eat or not eat. But I will emphasize the importance of what you choose to eat or not eat. Because what you eat, or do not eat, will, one hundred percent and without a doubt, have a direct impact on how you feel, not just physically, but mentally and emotionally as well. That is why I advocate for not avoiding but *embracing* food as an essential partner and helper on this journey.

When it comes to determining the best foods for you to consume—or avoid—I do not believe there is *any* one-size-fits-all answer. The answer to this question will be unique and personal to *you*. And this is where all the work we have done up until now, in learning how to sit still and listen, in tuning into our intuition and reconnecting with our bodies, comes into direct play. You will need to apply all of these tools and skills to navigating your own diet and what works best for you. Having said that, please do not underplay the importance of doing this work for yourself.

Now, back to the concept of "simple is beautiful." There are certain indisputable facts about nutrition that cut past all the diets and nutrition advice and systems and programs out there: If it's *real food,* if it comes directly from nature and from the earth, not heavily processed, refined or chemically altered, then it is probably a safe bet that it is nutritious for you. When we consume *real food*—that is, fresh produce and protein from animal or plants—then our bodies will receive the benefits of the nutrients packed inside those foods. In recovery, I find that the key to maintaining my health and my sanity is to keep it simple, focusing my nutritional intake on real food sources. However, I realize that implementing this can be easier said than done for those of us who live in a society that is heavily geared toward food that is convenient and fast. I'm not saying that it won't take some work, especially if we're used to fast food, but that doesn't mean that it has to be *hard*.

What's more, even if we stuff ourselves with kale and spinach, it can only offer as much benefit to our bodies as we are able to actually *absorb* the nutrients. Trauma takes a toll on every part of our systems, from the material world to the non-physical. This toll can play out in many ways and may be a little (or a lot) different for each survivor living with C-PTSD. That is why I do not believe there is any blanket approach to healing; rather, the only blanket approach we can apply is that we must each employ the necessary tools and skills to decode our own path of healing. The way the effects of trauma show up in your body will be specific to you and that will also inform how you approach your needs for physical rehabilitation.

When I got out of the high-control group, I quickly discovered just how badly off my body had become. You may not have been able to tell just by looking at me—aside, perhaps, from the haggard exhaustion worn into my face—but my nervous system and digestive system were in tatters. Physical health became one of my earliest focuses because it was impacting my ability to function, to think, to sleep…to *live*. I knew my body was seriously out of whack, but I didn't know where to begin to repair it. I tried eating healthy foods like salads and nutritious soups, but my stomach would gurgle and gurgle no matter what I ate. It seemed to reject nutrients. I certainly wasn't absorbing or feeling the benefits of all the nutrients available in even the healthiest of meals I consumed.

Out of desperation, I reached out to a nutritionist for a phone consultation. After listening to a description of my situation, she recommended a month-long program of getting back to the nutritional basics to begin resetting my digestive system while I ate only whole, natural foods. After a month, I would begin to gradually re-introduce more foods, monitoring how my body reacted to each one. This plan was not a diet. There was no caloric restriction; it was about eating lots of simple, nutrient-dense foods and alleviating as much workload from my digestive system as possible. In addition to the whole foods, I consumed a large quantity of supplements each morning and night that were designed to aid in the body's natural detoxification and nutrient synthesis processes.

After this month-long process, my body began gradually to repair itself. My stomach ceased its endless gurgling. My body felt stronger and more compact. My mind became clearer and I was able to concentrate better. It was a start.

While the dietary reset allowed me to reach a place of solid ground in terms of my physical state, it was just the beginning. It took time and practice listening to my body to determine what foods felt best after consuming. This discovery process will be unique for each of us. Restoring health, balance and energy to my body is an ongoing process. After two years of ongoing attention to this effort, I saw a marked increase in my energy, and medical labs indicated that my body was operating at high levels of health and functionality. For me, addressing my physical health was a top priority because of how deeply it was impacting my day-to-day life. Now that I was free, I wanted to be able to enjoy my life! It was clear that I would not be able to do that until I restored a basic level of vitality to my body.

Having said that, I think it's important to note that this is not a linear process. There are times when, due to stress, time constraints, financial constraints, trauma triggers, and a number of other factors, I find myself well off the wagon of consistently eating a healthful, real-food diet. I am doing my best, but it is not an all-or-nothing ride. There are periods of time when I succeed in my health goals more consistently than others, but the *overall trajectory* (which I can't highlight enough) is towards increasing levels of health and consistency. This is not about being perfect, my friend. And above all, this is NOT about *looking* a certain way. This is about reclaiming your body and all of its natural vibrancy, energy, health and physical ability so that you can live a full, meaningful and enjoyable life determined by your own free will.

If physical health is an area of challenge for you, I just want to say that I get it. The truth is, I believe it is an area of challenge for almost everyone, due to ongoing conflict between our society's focus on physical appearance and the massive pressure to indulge in the ease and convenience of fast, pre-packaged, heavily processed and comfort foods to ease the pain and confusion of it all. You are so not alone in this challenge.

The key is to find balance and to work towards that trajectory of increasing levels of health. You will accomplish this through *all* the practices and areas of recovery discussed in this book. Restoring and increasing health in our bodies through good nutrition and healthful physical activities is an ongoing, gradual process we must commit to engaging in for the rest of our lives. Balance is the key and balance is what we are striving for.

I am also an avid believer in the healing power of a good ol' bowl of ice cream, at the right time and place. I no longer support rigid, all-or-nothing, black-and-white thinking in any area of my life. I have experienced the profoundly healthful effects of baking a fresh batch of cookies. I don't advocate for sitting down and eating the entire batch at one time, but I love nothing more than to share my baked goods with others while enjoying them myself. I do not, for a second, believe that a cookie or an ice cream cone is bad for me—especially considering how much sheer joy I derive from indulging in these gifts—as long as I remember to partake of them in moderation and *not* to lean on them to substitute for self-love and self-care. That is when a good thing turns into dependency and addiction, which I have also experienced.

Finally, I want to point out one more thing: All the practices and exercises we have explored so far will also affect our bodies and our overall healing, even if they do not appear to be directly related to the body. Since our minds, hearts and bodies are indelibly linked, the work we do in each area will affect every other area. It is important to recognize that, while overhauling your physical health will improve your mental and emotional health to some degree, the reverse is also true. Neglecting any one of them will affect the others. I say this because I find that often, as humans, we tend toward focusing on one area more than the others—usually the area that is least intimidating to us. Unfortunately, just focusing on physical health, for example, is not a cure for comprehensive recovery. Each area requires its own attention, its own care and its own support in order for the whole to operate optimally.

A Note About Mental Nutrition

Yes, mental nutrition is a thing, too! We just don't think of it in those terms. But as it is with the body, so it is with the mind. I have learned to be careful about what ingredients I put into my mind. This comes in the form of media of all types: television, books, articles, social media, movies, music—you name it. What we put into our minds, consciously or unconsciously, will inform how we feel emotionally and physically, just as our physical health affects the mental and emotional state of being.

Over time, I have learned to pay attention to how I feel—physically and emotionally—after consuming some bit of media. My first experience of this occurred quite early in life, when I was just out of college. I'd gotten into a habit of watching a particular show on network TV on specific nights of the week (before we had Netflix and Smart TVs). When the show ended, the channel segued straight into the news while I lazily resisted the need to get up and get ready for bed. It didn't take me very long to discover the detrimental effects of watching the evening news before going to bed. It greatly impacted my mind and my sleep, in the worst of ways. Since then, I have learned that avoiding news media in general is essential to my health on all levels, but especially mentally and emotionally. I find that any important pieces of news still find their way to me without my ingesting copious amounts of fear and manipulation through the usual media outlets. When I do ingest news, I prefer to read it (which seems to involve fewer manipulative elements) and to seek it from as neutral a source as I can find.

In addition, there are some television shows that, while popular and acclaimed, I cannot watch because of the way I feel after viewing it. I may feel anxiety, a heaviness or sick feeling in my gut, a mood of fear or depression in my mind. There are a variety of possible outcomes. It can be very difficult to turn off a riveting show in the midst of an episode, but if I find that it consistently leaves me feeling bad or "off," I will simply not come back to it.

Honoring what feeds me *and* what pulls me down has been a lesson in self-love. As another example, I know that watching a horror movie is going to leave me feeling mentally and emotionally sick. They don't sit right with me and I can experience the effects of them even years later. Some people are lactose intolerant—I am horror intolerant. Therefore, I don't put myself in front of that media to begin with.

On the other hand, there are some forms of media that are good for me in moderation, but that I need to consume in smaller doses. As we'll discuss in the next chapter, educating myself on the systems of control that have been used against me most of my life has been a vital part of my recovery process. However, I cannot consume this content all day every day, or it will begin to drag me down mentally and emotionally, and therefore, physically as well. I've learned this through trial and error.

I might listen to a podcast on the topic of coercive control while I am cooking or cleaning and then move on to some fun music, for example. Or I may watch a documentary about a cult, or malignant narcissism, but then follow it up with an episode from a comedic show. This educational content, while valuable, can become the mental equivalent of overdosing on a medication if I binge it for too long. Too much of a good thing can be counterproductive.

Conversely, scrolling through social media reels for 15 minutes can be a fun, lighthearted diversion, often sprinkled in with some insightful thoughts, thanks to my current algorithm. My social media breaks are akin to that bowl of ice cream for my mind. When strategically consumed, these are a helpful boost to my mood and health, but when binged or over-consumed can have the exact opposite effect.

I hope this book can be an active example for you of mental nutrition. Feeding your mind with thoughts, insights, information and tools that bring healing, joy, peace and benefit to your life is the goal of mental nutrition. This can come in both serious and lighthearted ways. Never underestimate the power of a great comedy! Laughter is one of the most powerfully healing and nutritious supplements we can offer our body, mind and heart combined. It is a genuine medicine in and of itself. Mental nutrition makes us stronger, wiser, kinder and happier. If it doesn't offer any of these benefits, it's probably not a source that we want to allow much access into our lives.

The key here, as with food, is to find balance. Balance can be found through mindfulness. As you practice the tools and techniques from our first few chapters, they will further inform you in how to proceed in all aspects of nutrition. You will become increasingly aware of what helps you and what hurts, to what degree, and even at what times of the day, week, month or year.

So, What About Emotional Nutrition?

We've already covered a number of forms of emotional nutrition in this book, but let's take a moment to synthesize them here. When you think of emotional nutrition, think of what feeds goodness to your heart and spirit. What lifts you up? These are the activities and ideas that lead to optimal emotional health.

Deep connection, meaningful relationships and true love are some of the most nutrient-dense ingredients for emotional nutrition. Each of these ingredients start within *ourselves*. Building deep connection and creating a meaningful relationship with yourself and expressing true love for yourself is the key to vibrant emotional health. Yes, we can build and share these beautiful essentials with others as well, but first we must build them within ourselves. True emotional health is not dependent on anyone or anything outside of us. This is good news! This means that, to have strong emotional health, we don't have to wait for the right person or people to show up in our lives to experience connection or to feel true love. In fact, it will often happen the other way around.

So, how do you feed yourself those dense emotional nutrients?

- Practice sitting with yourself
- Allow yourself to feel what you are feeling
- Suspend self-judgment and harsh criticism; silence that inner critic
- Practice listening to your heart and *acting* on it
- Be kind to yourself
- Speak with, and to, yourself with gentleness, understanding, respect and love
- Be patient with yourself
- Spend time with yourself doing things you love
- Practice self-care through creating a comfortable environment (See Chapters 4 & 6)
- Be kind and nurturing to your body.

All of the steps we have covered so far are aspects of emotional care for building strong emotional health. However, there are a couple of other key components that will enable you to build radical emotional health in record time. One of them we've only touched on so far…

Emotional Superfood #1
Gratitude

Do any research on happiness that you like and the one most consistent and key concept that comes up over and over is the power of Gratitude. This one essential element seems to be the cornerstone of human emotional health, happiness and peace. I would be remiss not to give this ingredient its full due here.

If you want to fast-track your emotional health and overall sense of happiness, gratitude is the way. I first discovered the power of gratitude when I was in my mid-twenties. I'll take you back to that time to describe how it happened.

When I reached a real low at the age of twenty-five—the lowest point of my life to that date—out of sheer desperation, I started researching how to be happy. Yes, I took to analytically researching this topic because of my prolonged, unrelenting depression. As I did, gratitude was the first idea I encountered. I took note, but I kept researching. Gratitude felt like too high of a hill to climb in that moment. As I continued my research, however, it was the one idea that came up over and over and over again, no matter where I looked: self-help, psychology, spirituality, physical science—you name it, gratitude was there. I quickly deduced that I needed to take this concept to heart if I was serious about becoming a happy person.

The first brick wall I came up against was, "What do I have to be grateful for?" When you've been anxious and depressed for the better part of your life, you have no money, you see no future for yourself, you believe you've failed at pursuing the only dreams that ever made you feel alive, and you are utterly alone...well, it can seem quite the challenge to find things to be *grateful* for. But two of my most questionable characteristics when combined—stubbornness and determination—can also be put to positive use when I choose. In this case, I committed myself to finding something, *anything*, to be grateful for.

If you find yourself in a similar situation, I urge you to start small. Very small. You can start on a minute level. What I learned is that it doesn't matter *what* you are grateful for—all that matters is finding a pinhole to get you through to the *feeling* of gratitude. That is what we are going for. That is where the secret gate code to happiness lies.

When I found myself lying on my bed in tears, thinking I had literally nothing to be grateful for in that moment, wracking my brain for just *one good thing* in my life...it eventually dawned on me that, in that very same moment, I was sitting in my favorite place to be: my bed. I loved my bed. It was where I felt safe. It was where I could be warm in the midst of a frozen winter. It was soft and inviting and the only place I could completely let down my walls and just *be*. My bed. That was the first thing I came up with to feel grateful for, as silly or crazy or stupid as that might sound. But you know what? It worked. I focused on my feelings of gratitude for my bed and the safe space it provided me. As I did so, they grew. The feelings of safety and warmth and appreciation and relaxation intensified right then and there. I got my first taste of the gentle, warm happiness that comes with the feeling of genuine gratitude.

This practice required me to focus on the smallest of things at first, whatever I could find: my morning cup of coffee, the cute little messages on the sugar packets I used to sweeten my cup each day, the quiet and stillness of those early morning moments by myself. I focused on this experience with gratitude in my heart and it became a sacred morning ritual, a way to start my day with a little slice of happiness. I also continued to express this gratitude within myself at night when I returned to the warmth, safety and softness of my bed, ending my day with another little taste of happiness in my heart.

To this day, the deep satisfaction and pleasure I receive from these simple daily rituals—at the start of my day and at the end of it—has never left me. It was that impactful. From there, it was just a matter of finding more and more things to feel grateful for. Once you get a taste of the experience of gratitude, how it feels in your heart and your body, it becomes easier and easier to find sources for gratitude all around you, all day long. It just takes a little practice, but it's actually the easiest thing in the world.

In the trauma recovery process, gratitude can be the life preserver that saves your mind, heart and body. While it may seem difficult or daunting at first to find something to be grateful for, I urge you, once again, to start small. It's amazing the things that we take for granted until they are gone. Simple pleasures that come through our senses. Having physical senses at all. You must find your own pinhole to happiness through the gateway of gratitude, using the simplest, smallest thing you can find in your inner or outer world. I promise you it exists. Be determined to find out. Then you will discover how much more there is.

Once you get a taste of the power of gratitude, you will almost certainly want more. Unless, that is, you prefer feeling miserable and hopeless. (Although I jest, some of us really do! Some of us find it safer there.) You can get as radical with gratitude as you choose. I have gone so far as to find sources for gratitude within my experiences of trauma. And I genuinely feel it. For me, it has been a vital part of my healing process. Learning to find silver linings—sources for gratitude—in every single part of our lives is a skill that requires cultivating.

"How on earth could you *ever* be grateful for the hellish experiences you have been through?" I have been asked. The answer is that I'm not. I'm not grateful for the abuse or the pain. But I *am* grateful for the perspective and the deep lessons they have brought me. The truth is, there is a depth, an emotional intelligence and a capacity for empathy and understanding that can be found among trauma survivors, and which I find within myself, for which I am deeply grateful. There are deep understandings to be gained about life, about others and about ourselves, if we choose to use our experiences to that end.

At the beginning of my recovery process, I determined that I wanted to somehow use my worst life experiences for good, to give them some positive meaning in the world, and that has been my goal ever since. I don't know if I would have the drive, or the capacity, to hold space for others and their own pain if I hadn't endured the pain of my past. I am most genuinely grateful for the insight, the wisdom and the perspective that it has afforded me. Finally, I have a great appreciation for my life now, and I often see that the abundant and simple joys a free life has to offer go unnoticed, or taken for granted, by those who have not experienced the darkness and pain from a life of trauma. The freedom I now have to experience and live my life the way that I choose feels like a great gift and an incredible luxury. As the saying goes, "you don't know what you got 'til it's gone." My past, and all that pain, can now be transmuted into the source of great joy, pleasure and appreciation. For that, I am *grateful.*

I realize this may not be a popular opinion, so I want to make one thing super clear. I am not urging you to send a "thank you" note to your abuser (or perform the mental equivalent). What I am suggesting is that we can be grateful for the unique perspective our experiences provide us and that we can be extremely grateful for the opportunity to break free from that life and start anew. We can be grateful for all the gifts that life is presenting us now by taking a few moments of our day to seek out those little treasures and acknowledge them, fostering the opportunity to see and experience even more of the goodness that our post-trauma life may provide.

We are not taught to see our trauma through this lens, but the truth is, it can become your personal superpower. Your life now, and your commitment to your recovery, is a testament to your strength, your capability, your resilience and your wisdom. Use it accordingly. This can be a silver lining found around your darkest days, if you so choose.

Emotional Superfood #2
Extending Care to Others

Your decision to do the work of recovery, to heal yourself, is in fact a gift to all others as well. Each of us who chooses to use our path and our life to bring more love, kindness, light and healing to the world, even just through bringing those elements into our own lives, is offering healing to the entire universe. Every choice we make impacts the whole. Even if your motivations for healing are entirely selfish, the reality is that the impact will be globally beneficial.

To supercharge your emotional health and personal happiness storehouse, there is another secret ingredient that, like gratitude, will catapult your well-being into new heights of health. This ingredient is also profoundly simple. It is helping others. You want to feel good? Make someone else feel good. You want to help yourself? Help someone else. It is truly that simple.

The recovery process can be extremely self-centered. This is not only necessary but it is *right,* because the work starts within *ourselves.* I want to take a moment to stress here the importance of prioritizing self-care first. The recommendation I am offering to you below comes later in this book, and in this process, on purpose. That is because all too often in our prior lives, we have become habituated to self-sacrifice, tending to others, and considering our own needs last, if at all. This mode is usually part of survival and is not the heart-centered level of giving that we will discuss below. In order for us to help others in a productive, healing and meaningful way, we must first become proficient at truly caring for ourselves, comfortable with setting healthy boundaries and confident in our ability to say "no" when that is right for us. Until we have mastered this level of self-care, extending care to others will likely remain problematic and not offer the benefits that we are discussing here.

Extending love and care toward ourselves is primary. Tending to our basic needs as well as to our mental, emotional and spiritual repair must come first. Once we've begun to get the hang of taking good care of ourselves, the next step—and the one that will really have the greatest impact of all—is to begin to extend that work outward. To think of others, to assist others, to offer kindness, support and care for others is the culmination of true self-help.

We are not talking about self-sacrifice here. You don't have to give it all up and become Mother Theresa to effect meaningful change in the world. In fact, you may feel as if you have nothing at all to offer anyone else. While it can feel this way, and most certainly does when we are fresh out of a traumatic experience, it is factually untrue.

Have you ever felt the warmth of a genuine smile from a stranger? Felt the camaraderie of a shared laugh or a knowing look between you and someone you don't know? Benefited from a kind word from a passerby? If you have, then you know first-hand the power of such a simple moment. These moments remind us that we are connected and not alone. They lift our spirits and brighten our life ever so slightly, but we often brush them off or take them for granted. However, I have had simple moments like these turn my entire day around when I've been in the throes of post-trauma loneliness and isolation.

If you want to help others and positively affect the world, but you don't know how, start small. The key here is putting conscious intention behind finding opportunities to spread kindness and care. Start by offering the kind of energy to others that you would like to receive yourself. As someone who has worked in customer service for decades, I can attest to the fact that your energy *does* matter and it *does* affect other people, for better or for worse, even those whom you may not see or speak to in person. We are responsible for the impact we are having on the world, whether we're conscious of it or not. I encourage you to be conscious of it, because that same impact comes directly back to us. We tend to receive energy matching that which we give out.

Offer a bit of encouragement to someone who seems down. Greet a stranger warmly. Provide some assistance to someone who is struggling. Verbally express the complimentary thought you just had about that person, whether you know them or not. Engage in random acts of kindness. You have no way of knowing the long-term impacts of these simple gestures. In some cases, moments like this have changed the trajectory of someone's entire life. Best of all, these simple acts will not only spread love into the world around you, they will make *you* feel amazing too! We can help ourselves profoundly by helping others.

If and when you receive the inspiration to help the world in other ways, I urge you to act on them as soon as possible. Inspiration is a tricky thing. It can come in a flash, and if we don't act on it, it can disappear just as quickly, along with our motivation. It took me more than four decades to finally learn that inspiration only continues to flow when we grab it by the horns, hang on with all our might and choose to ride it all the way to the end of the road. When we seize inspiration (rather than overlooking it, putting it off for a better time, making a note of it and then forgetting about it, etc.), not only does the original inspiration grow, morph and evolve, but it invites in a host of new inspirations for us to seize.

Finding ways to help others and to serve the world is essential to feeling purposeful. Conversely, feeling purposeful is essential to leading a fulfilling and happy life. Extending care to others is a mindset that we can intentionally cultivate, and in so doing, we will naturally discover more opportunities to do so. As we do, we organically feed our own emotional health and fulfillment. What a beautiful cycle, huh? Who knew that emotional nutrition was such a deep and underrated aspect of life?

8

Educating Yourself on Systems of Control

One of the toughest aspects of living with C-PTSD, in my opinion, is the sense of isolation it creates. This isolation is borne of the unique consequences of carrying the weight of your experiences in a way that can subtly or deeply affect you in any given moment, sometimes in predictable ways, but often in unforeseen ways. Long-term trauma survivors seem to feel uniquely alone because, even when they do have close companions or relationships in their lives, if those others don't share their experience, it can be a source of separation. Even though we don't want this to be the case, there is no way to give someone else the full understanding, not only of what you have experienced, but of how that experience is impacting you on a moment-to-moment basis.

The isolation of post-trauma can be excruciating. Not only have I experienced it firsthand, but I have also witnessed survivors in close, long-term, committed relationships who still experience the frustrating isolation of their ongoing post-trauma recovery within those relationships. It is not necessarily because our friends, families or significant others don't want to understand us or because they are doing anything wrong. There is simply a limit to what can be understood and shared without the context of firsthand experience. While this may sound exclusionary, or even arrogant to some, I have witnessed and experienced it all too often in my time of recovery, so I think it is an ugly truth we must face during this process.

This isolation is one of the reasons why I believe that trauma recovery education is such an important aspect of our healing journey. Another reason education plays such a critical role is that it is a key to preventing us from repeating history and winding up in similar situations. Educating ourselves on the influences and intricacies that created the circumstances of our former lives helps us to spot those red flags and the "wolves in sheep's clothing" in the future. Education is power.

When I ended up in the office of the narcissistic life coach who eventually took over my entire life through more than a decade of gradual and methodical indoctrination, coercion, grooming and manipulation, I landed there because I was looking to heal from the first eighteen years of my life. During those initial formative years, I lived under the total control of a dictatorial and narcissistic father who wielded his puritanical power with the approval of a radical religious belief system and the support of its community. With that early experience, I should have been able to spot the danger of that life coach from a mile away, right?

Not at all. I did not have the resources, the understanding, the education, or the knowledge to recognize what I was seeing. This life coach used a completely different language, and entirely new spiritual concepts, from that of my upbringing. He didn't look or sound like my father at all. In fact, he wholeheartedly validated that my childhood was wrought with abuse and dysfunction. He advocated for a path of healing down which he was eager to escort me. I had never heard of love bombing, at that point. I knew nothing of malignant narcissism. Complex PTSD, coercive control and cult recovery were nowhere in the mainstream vernacular of society. Instead of seeing the red flags, I found comfort in the familiarity of this man's authoritarianism and intimidating, controlling presence. But please understand, I did not recognize that *consciously*. That subconscious programming is how trauma and indoctrination work and how it can inform our decisions in unseen ways. Due to my early conditioning, compounded by the effects of unhealed trauma, I was *perfect prey*.

Hindsight is 20/20.

When I finally escaped the life coach fourteen years later, I delved headlong into research and education. I sank my teeth into documentaries, books, podcasts, organizations, YouTube videos, cult expert consultations—all the things. I happened to escape my cultic nightmare within a couple of years of the "big bang" of cult awareness hitting the main stream media. NXIVM, which became known as the "Hollywood Sex Cult" (an unfair and reductive description of this destructive organization), imploded just a few years before and the documentary detailing that event was making waves and shining a light on these types of groups. Cults had the full attention of the zeitgeist, as they continue to do now, so information and media were exploding in every direction. I've heard it said that we are living in the Golden Age of Cult Recovery. I believe this assessment is accurate, because there is more information, support and resources for survivors of high-control groups and narcissistic relationships now than ever before, and it is easier than ever to access it.

None of these resources were so readily accessible in the early 2000s when I first emerged from the culty confines of my childhood. More importantly, I did not have enough awareness or understanding of the trauma I was attempting to process to know how to look for these resources. I just thought something was terribly wrong with *me*. I knew the way I was raised was suspect, but like a fish trying to see water, it is difficult to see the severity of issues objectively when that is all you have ever known. In my earliest attempts to process my childhood, the psychologists I visited regarded me as if I were a mythic two-headed hydra and proceeded to take notes furiously as I spoke. I felt more like a circus side-show than a patient who could be helped. No one ever spoke to me about religious abuse, cultic abuse, religious trauma, family cults, narcissistic personality disorder, gaslighting, love bombing or *any* of these topics which are becoming front and center in the world of complex trauma recovery today.

Fast forward to present day. Books, articles, podcasts, Ted Talks, documentaries, audio books and YouTube videos abound. Regardless of the specifics of your past, your trauma and your recovery journey, there is a wealth of information available to help you understand how the systems of influence, power and control work in abusive groups, families and organizations. It's time to whip out your computer or your mobile device and start digging. Do your own investigations and research, specific to your interests and challenges, utilizing all the sources that are available to us in this Information Age. The more we understand about how we ended up in our specific situations, the better equipped we are to prevent ourselves and others from repeating the lessons of our past. Not only that, but as we uncover these insights about how we were controlled and abused, this knowledge alone can offer some incredibly healing revelations and absolution.

I am so grateful to have all of these resources at my fingertips on this second go at escaping cultic abuse. These resources have revolutionized the recovery process for me—a process I never had the chance to begin on my first attempt to get clarity and heal. This time, I am determined not to fall prey to another abusive person, relationship or organization again. This means educating myself thoroughly and continuously. It means elevating myself to the top of the proverbial food chain to become prey no more.

Survivor Stories

Learning about the systems of control, influence, power and abuse behind your experience is the first step. There are many ways to do this. How you choose to go about it, and which resources you tap into first, should be informed by your particular experience and background. Due to the overwhelming confusion and isolation that survivors experience when they step out of the prison they've been in, I recommend delving into firsthand accounts of other survivors who share a similar background to yours. This can be incredibly helpful, as you learn that you are so not alone in what you have been through, and also, you see how others have managed to carry on, and perhaps, to heal a bit.

Initially, I immersed myself in all things cult. As I progressed in my education, however, I discovered that my experience and the lasting impact it was having on my daily life shared vast similarities with survivors of all kinds of varying backgrounds who had experienced very different forms of abuse from mine. An important point I have learned is that, while forms of abuse may vary widely, the effects are similar for all survivors, regardless of their specific experience. It is this unique thread of commonality that binds us together. Consequently, survivors seem to share a unique language that they understand innately, even if their experiences and circumstances are drastically different.

I have heard stories of survivors who endured brutal physical violence from their own parents, women who have been victims of sex trafficking schemes, young women who have been coerced into relationships where they endured sexual and physical torture, survivors of off-the-grid extremist religious groups, children raised in end-of-days family cults, and the list goes on and on and on. In every single one of these cases, in their accounts of their experiences and the struggles they face as a result of them, I find identical components and experiences to my own. At the end of the day, abuse is abuse, trauma is trauma and human suffering is human suffering. I have learned so much from every single one of these brave warriors who have chosen to share their stories, their perspectives and their hearts. They have helped me to feel less alone, a little seen and a little heard. They have inspired me. They have helped me to heal.

In this Golden Age of Trauma Recovery, books abound—from memoirs to educational tomes to healing handbooks such as this one. Audio books are a lifesaver for me; they have enabled me to readily find and absorb these materials. A common side effect of complex trauma is that some of the physical alterations that occur in the brain during long periods of coercion and control inhibit one's ability to sit and focus on a task for extended periods, such as reading. In my first months out, I was unable to read for more than fifteen minutes at a time. However, as I continue to rebuild that muscle, I have discovered that listening to books is something I can easily do as I'm getting dressed for the day, driving on my commute, cooking, or going about daily chores.

In addition to books, documentaries and podcasts are exploding in every direction. If you prefer to watch your stories, there is no shortage of media covering survivor stories of all kinds. When I escaped my small spirituality-based therapy group in the summer of 2022 with three other members of the group, we were extremely fortunate to reconnect with a former member of our group who had gotten out two years earlier. She'd spent those two years diving headfirst into cult recovery education while the rest of us stayed mired in the group, and it was thanks to the resources she passed along to us in our first weeks out that I was able to begin my education process so early. I watched the NXIVM documentary *The Vow* in those first few months of my liberation and it was transformative. That documentary put my own experience in a certain framework that made the truth of our little group undeniable. I was shocked at just how similar the content of that large-scale cult was to the small group I'd just left. The full reality of my situation became clear much faster than it otherwise would have as I began to absorb these materials and give specific language and context to my experiences.

I quickly came to learn that coercive controllers and abusers are all operating from the same playbook. They are all utilizing the *same* techniques, the *same* tricks, the *same* tactics and the *same* tools to manipulate, control, con and abuse. As I read other survivors' accounts and watched documentaries, I discovered that other people had undergone the exact same forms of abuse, humiliation and punishment that I had endured. I watched footage of leaders from entirely different groups spout the *exact same rhetoric* that my leader had presented to us—word for word.

It was difficult for me to see this at first. Accepting this reality meant I had to accept the truth that I had trusted and devoted myself to a person who was consciously and intentionally choosing to manipulate, exploit, and control me from day one. I could offer no excuses or benefit of the doubt to my former leader, the person I unwittingly handed over 14 years of my life to.

Waking up to the reality that you have been conned is a hard pill to swallow; the initial shock leaves you frozen, your mind running back over every conversation and decision, searching for the moments when you could have rewritten your history. There's a heaviness in your chest and a gnawing ache in your stomach as you realize how your trust was twisted and used against you. You question your own judgment and sanity, feeling both betrayed and bewildered, and wonder how you missed the warning signs that now seem so obvious in hindsight. The realization sinks in slowly and in stages, accompanied by disbelief and a sense of vulnerability that is difficult to shake.

Despite this new awareness, all those convictions and beliefs that I cultivated over years of wholehearted loyalty and dedication to a leader and cause that initially appeared to be worthy of all my energy and attention did not disappear overnight. That is the power of indoctrination and that is why deconstruction takes time. The more education I received, the less denial I could hold for the reality of what I had experienced and the intentional manipulation that had been used to indoctrinate me. As it turns out, nothing about my experience, or what my leader managed to do in our little therapy group, was original in any way.

There is a joke in the cult recovery world that all cult leaders seem to have been given the same "messiah's handbook." As I continue to meet other real-life survivors and hear their own tales, I am shocked over and over again at the similarity of our experiences. It is deeply affirming to know that I am not alone in this process and to be able to definitively name my experience. After all, when we are able to give language to that dark thing hiding in the shadows, to give a name to our traumatic experience, it takes some of the power and mystery away from that shadowy monster. It gives that power back to *us*.

Finding Support

Connecting with other survivors is another key tool in the self-education and healing process. For many of us, this is a scary step, but it can also be a highly rewarding one. Thanks to the resources provided by the former member of my own little group who escaped a couple of years earlier, I was introduced to organizations and individuals whose whole purpose was providing support for survivors of groups like mine, both large and small. These resources and connections continue to offer me ongoing support in my recovery journey. I learned about, and joined, a world of virtual support groups that bring individuals together from all over the world with this shared background. I learned that my experience was more common than I ever could have imagined.

Taking the first step to join one of these groups, or to attend your first gathering, is a brave move. It can be intimidating to walk into any room full of strangers, much less a room of strangers who are all there for the communal purpose of connecting and sharing about the darkest and most traumatic experiences of their lives. However, this purpose creates an atmosphere of comfort and camaraderie. For once, you are in a room where every person present can relate with one another on a level that we may not experience in our day-to-day lives.

Having said that, for any support group to be truly helpful, it must be safe. For survivors of cultic abuse, the nature of a support group can be tricky, depending on the circumstances and practices of your particular cultic group or narcissistic relationship. It is essential that you go into any group with an open mind but also with a commitment to your personal boundaries. A safe support group will never push you to share anything that you do not wish or to engage beyond the limits of what is comfortable for you.

The support groups I have attended have all required the new member to be vetted by the host or organizers of the group prior to coming. This is a safety measure to ensure that all attendees are there for the same purposes and have similar goals and intentions for joining. If you reach out to attend a group and they require this step to be taken first, that is a positive sign. Virtual meetings are typically not recorded and should never be recorded without the awareness and consent of every person in attendance.

A safe support group will present a space that is free of judgment, free of agenda and free of unsolicited advice. It is wise to assess a group that you are joining for the first time to make sure it meets these criteria, and to make sure it presents an open, accepting atmosphere for you. Joining a group for the first time (or even second or third) may not be comfortable, but it is important to discern the difference between feeling *discomfort* and feeling *unsafe* as you proceed down your personal path of recovery. There are many uncomfortable steps that must be taken in our healing journey, but we should never be pushing ourselves into something that is unsafe—an important difference to distinguish for those of us who have often barreled past our healthy boundaries and the red flags of that which is unsafe, due to the coercion and manipulation of our cultic groups.

There are also survivor book clubs and writing groups, which are both great resources for connecting with others while educating yourself, processing your experiences and tapping into a healing place of creativity. The same general rules apply. You should feel safe in these environments and always be treated with respect. In my experience, circles with other survivors are one of the most open, understanding and accepting places you can find yourself. Finding a group that feels right for you can be a huge asset on your healing journey.

Pitfalls to Avoid in the Survivor Circle

Many survivors struggle to call their experience what it was. For a lot of us, there is a tendency to downplay our particular situation or to feel like an imposter among others whom we believe had it worse than us. We share that human tendency to judge and compare, deeming others "better" than us, even in the comparison of traumas. Your own experience is all you know, so it may not seem as weighty or significant as someone else's story seems to you. On the other hand, you may encounter the opposite issue. You may feel that someone else's experience is trivial compared to your own and feel annoyance with their reaction to their "lesser" trauma.

I warn you of these reactions because I have not only seen them, I have fallen on both sides of this line at different points. There are times where I felt particularly slighted by life due to the experiences I have endured, resenting those who I felt traveled less difficult paths. Other times, I have greatly downplayed the extent and severity of my own experiences in light of other people's shocking stories of abuse and survival. While I think it is inherently human to feel the draw toward these judgments, I have discovered time and again that neither stance is true. So, beware the pitfall of comparison.

Remember, trauma is not actually the distressing event that occurred; rather, it is the human *response* to the distressing event which overwhelmed our ability to cope with it. Trauma is the *result* in our minds, bodies and hearts—the tear in the fabric of our being that we now endure, caused by our inability to process what occurred, and which we now undertake to mend. That is why two people can undergo the same event or circumstances and yet walk away from it with very different interpretations or long-term effects.

As in any other area of the world, egos abound in trauma recovery circles as well. The goal of a healthy and safe support group is not to see who has the bigger trauma story or who has the best chances at a movie deal. I urge you not to get caught up in these comparisons or even the most subtle trauma competitions. A basic understanding of trauma reveals just how impossible it is to compare.

Most importantly of all, please remember that *you* are the captain of your own recovery ship. There are many experts in the field of trauma, narcissism and cultic abuse, but even this field is not immune to narcissistic predators. Although they may first appear as benevolent authorities within the fields of healing and recovery, it is always important to run every bit of guidance and every new relationship through your own internal intuitive system. Many malignant narcissists gravitate toward fields that gain them external authority and inspire trust, such as the fields of medicine, therapy and clergy. It is important to remember that trust must be built and earned, regardless of someone's position or title. No one knows better than you what you need.

Having said all that, support groups can be an effective way to process some of your experiences and to find camaraderie with others who understand and relate to your story. The telling of our stories can be a powerful catalyst for healing, much like writing in a journal can be a method for catharsis. Emptying ourselves of these painful pasts which we tend to conceal in secrecy allows fresh air and light to come in and disinfect those wounds. Sometimes we don't even realize how much shame we have built up around these stories which we hold inside of us.

I had the great fortune of meeting some truly beautiful souls through survivor support groups. Their stories, their encouragement and their open, unabashed seeing of me has been vital to my recovery process. The emotional depth and intelligence I find in a group of trauma survivors is unmatched. This is not a place for idle chit chat and long discussions on the weather; these are the places where the deepest, brightest and most bitter parts of life can be seen and held with grace.

The Suffering of Man

Despite what we tend to believe, there is no real comparison when it comes to human suffering. Viktor Frankl immaculately explains this concept in his book *Man's Search for Meaning,* in which he partly recounts his three years spent in Nazi concentration camps during World War II. Frankl writes:

> A man's suffering is similar to the behavior of gas. If a certain quantity of gas is pumped into an empty chamber, it will fill the chamber completely and evenly, no matter how big the

> chamber. Thus, suffering completely fills the human soul and conscious mind, no matter whether the suffering is great or little.

Seeking Therapy

Part of the self-education process is learning about the healing process. Reading (or listening to) books about trauma recovery can offer invaluable tools, insights and techniques to aid us on our journey. Then there's learning about the systems of control which formerly imprisoned us by absorbing information, watching documentaries and listening to speakers explain how narcissistic abuse, cultic control and sociopathy operate in a variety of contexts. These are all helpful ways to empower and arm ourselves as we not only deconstruct our own experiences but navigate the path ahead of us, searching to build healthy relationships and healthy environments within which to lead our new lives. Things get significantly more real and personal when we engage with others, hearing the firsthand truths and struggles of survivor journeys while sharing our own. We can then begin to apply all this knowledge we've been collecting in a more personal way.

The most intense aspect of self-education occurs when we begin to actively study ourselves: our patterns, our desires, what drives us and what holds us back. In the first chapters, we explored the importance of rebuilding our relationship with ourselves and techniques to do that. I believe that reconnecting with our inner world and our true mind is the most important part of the recovery process and the one we will engage in for the rest of our lives.

Another tool that can be helpful in this process of self-discovery and reconnection is therapy. In therapy, we have the opportunity to do that healing work with the aid of a skilled observer. A good therapist is a like a nurse who assists in attending to our wounds and immediate needs while we are the doctors who do the intensive work of healing within ourselves. The assistance of that nurse can be vital in times of crisis, when all the alarms are sounding off, and they can be a source of comfort in the times of recovery between procedures.

It took me more than two years after I got out to commit to seeking a therapist to assist in my recovery journey. Since a significant amount of the abuse I endured was under the pretense of "therapy," and took place in a space that was designed to mimic the therapeutic environment, I needed time to rebuild the connection within myself, to my own mind and heart, to feel safe enough to enter into a therapeutic relationship with a genuine, licensed therapist. Although I recognized the need for therapy, and even desired it, I needed to know that I could hear and would trust my own mind, heart and intuition over the guidance or influence of any outside source before I could safely and confidently commit myself to seeking therapy.

Once I reached that point, I still had to face the challenge of finding a therapist, setting up appointments, and managing all the logistics of starting therapy. As those suffering from trauma will be uniquely and intimately aware, some of life's most mundane tasks can be simply too overwhelming for us to complete. Making a phone call, navigating to a place we've never been before, setting up an appointment, performing a new task—these relatively small to-do's can be so mountainous to our traumatized brains that we simply won't do them. On top of that, many of us are faced with the difficulty of figuring out how to financially afford therapy. I was only able to begin considering therapy once I received medical insurance benefits from my workplace, for the first time in my life, which finally made therapy a possibility. I felt extremely fortunate to have benefits that would cover the cost of these services, but they also added an extra layer of challenge in navigating the world of medical insurance and available therapists who might be able to meet my specific needs within those constraints.

Like finding a safe support group, it is equally vital that we find safe therapists to work with during trauma recovery. Narcissists abound in the therapeutic field, unfortunately, because it is an excellent avenue through which to gain undue influence over others. Therefore, it is essential that you use all your wits, intuition and discernment when working with a therapist. Not only should they be licensed and credentialed, but they must be a good fit for *you.*

Most therapists will offer a free consultation to discuss your needs, answer any questions, and determine if you are a good fit for one another prior to beginning a therapeutic relationship. I urge you to make full use of this consultation to ask frank questions. It is your time to interview the therapist and learn about their background, their credentials, and what types of therapeutic approaches they employ in their practice. This is a great time to ask whether they have any special training in trauma recovery, whether they are familiar with the needs of clients dealing with C-PTSD and how they approach those needs. A good therapist will welcome your candid inquiries and be forthcoming with their answers. Unfortunately, most therapists do not yet have extensive knowledge or training in the needs of clients coping with C-PTSD and the niche arena of cult recovery. However, you may find a therapist who is open and willing to educate themselves in these areas in order to better assist you. There are books and classes available to mental health professionals who choose to pursue specialized training in these matters.

A safe therapist will respect your boundaries, listen to you and feel comfortable for you to talk to. That is not to say that all your conversations will be comfortable, but as with a support group, they must feel *safe*. A good therapist will be there to help you for as long as you need, without the goal of keeping you under their "care" indefinitely. A good therapist will work with you toward reaching your own clear and finite goals. A good therapist will help you to work toward the point of not needing their help anymore…until the next time you do.

Your goals for therapy will be unique to you and will inform the therapist you choose. For myself, I needed a space to talk freely. I needed a place free of judgment and influence to tell my story and get it out of me. I needed an objective sounding board to witness me and offer intelligent feedback. I needed to put words to the things that felt horrible and shameful within myself and to see if my judgments were true and rational. I needed a safe, consistent outlet for all the thoughts, memories and emotions churning within me. I needed someone to assist me in deconstructing my experiences, the indoctrination that continues to impact my life and the means of coercion which were used to manipulate, groom and control me. I am still actively seeking assistance in the therapeutic space.

The work of therapy is the work of educating ourselves *about ourselves*. It is a place where we go to do the deep, exploratory work of seeing our patterns, taking responsibility for the parts of our life that we can control, perhaps facing an inner demon or two and healing old wounds, all with a trusty sidekick there to support us and have our back in the process. It is not a passive thing, the process of healing. It is intentional, active, sometimes gory and incomparably rewarding. We receive benefit from it in proportion to the effort we put into it.

A therapist is not required to do this inner work, however. For some of us, therapy may not be an option, whether due to financial constraints, personal or trauma-induced barriers to it, or simply the difficulty of finding a good therapeutic fit given your specific needs and background. I found that it can be incredibly challenging to find a therapist who has the knowledge, tools and background to assist in C-PTSD recovery, or who is willing to do the extra working of training themselves in it. A wide variety of prohibitive factors may limit or prevent your ability to find a therapist, but I believe it can be a valuable tool in the healing journey if or when a good fit can be found. If therapy is not an option for you, do not distress. Like so many others, I have faced the challenge of therapizing myself and that is a very real route for many trauma survivors. The tools, techniques and resources offered in this book are intended to assist you in doing just that, if necessary.

Flooding & Boundaries

In the earliest days of recovery, when we are still reeling, we may find ourselves sharing more about ourselves and our story than we might otherwise intend. In addition, sharing our stories or listening to others' stories (among other triggers), can evoke a reaction known as flooding, in which you may feel completely overwhelmed by emotions and memories. In some cases, flooding and oversharing collide into a dynamic duo that, on the receiving end, may feel like trauma dumping. On the giving end, you may feel raw, extra vulnerable, exposed, anxious or ashamed afterward.

Oversharing and flooding are common pitfalls to be aware of in the process of trauma recovery. I have been on both the giving and the receiving end of these behaviors. Sometimes, when you begin to crack the seal of a lid you've been keeping on so tight, the pressure release feels uncontainable. If you find yourself flooded with memories or emotions and oversharing, it can be incredibly difficult to stop it in the moment. It may feel like an uncontrollable force spilling out of you. It is wise to spend some time getting to know others before divulging all your innermost thoughts, feeling and experiences with them, so being conscious of your particular triggers to flood and overshare is helpful in navigating new relationships.

When we are just learning how to interact and build new relationships after experiencing relational trauma, we are also learning how to set healthy and appropriate personal boundaries. These boundaries may have been nonexistent in our previous lives. In my group, for example, healthy boundaries were interpreted as "ego limitations" which were designed to keep us separate. That was considered a bad thing, so we were actively coerced into destroying those boundaries for the purpose of "returning to unity and wholeness."

It is taking time for me to find a new, healthy balance between connecting with others while not divulging my entire life story to someone I've just met. At first, I was so out of balance in this area that I thought I was being deceptive to withhold any information about myself. I actually felt as if I were lying to new acquaintances by not sharing the personal details of my life right out the gate; that's how foreign personal boundaries had become and how I was indoctrinated to believe I was not entitled to have them. Despite that inner conflict, I ultimately chose to exercise patience and withhold many personal details until I had adequate time and space to assess the safety of new surroundings and determine who I could trust with more personal information.

These boundaries are especially vital in the beginning because we are so vulnerable at this early stage of recovery. We may not yet be able to successfully discern safe new people from those who might gain these deeper insights about our lives to manipulate or exploit us, whether intentionally or not. I now think of my personal sharing as something that has to be earned. I need to feel a sense of safety and I must have a sense that the other person has earned this level of intimacy from me. It is no longer freely given. Building and respecting your own boundaries is the best way to prevent inappropriate levels of oversharing. Boundaries are the floodgates that keep the tumult of water contained as needed.

A session with a safe therapist or trusted friend is the ideal time to allow flooding thoughts, feelings and memories to flow out of you, if possible. When you're aware of what flooding is, you are more likely to recognize when it is happening. If you find it happening in a less than ideal or unvetted space, just pump the brakes as soon as you are able to. Do *not* shame or berate yourself for it—it happens to the best of us. You have not done anything wrong; it is simply an opportunity to exert your self-care and self-protection skills. Just do your best to be mindful, come back into the present moment and perhaps make a mental note that you may benefit from some journaling or free writing soon. Take an opportunity to sit down with yourself or with a safe person, and allow whatever needs to come out of you to flow freely.

9

Connection in the Life After

One of the greatest challenges I face in my newfound freedom is establishing a new community. While boundaries were being eliminated between those within our small group, we were paradoxically encouraged to "set healthy boundaries" by limiting or severing contact with relationships deemed toxic outside of the group. Those relationships deemed to be unhealthy or holding us back typically stemmed from family relations or old friends from our former lives who were not electing to join us on this path of spiritual pursuits.

After years of slowly slipping into isolation due to all that disconnecting and severing of former relationships, reentering mainstream society has been a lonely endeavor. I am one of the few very lucky people to have left my group *with* other members of my group, which is a great blessing. Many of us getting out of high control groups or relationships must do so entirely on our own, foregoing all former connections and relationships from that part of our lives. Such a feat requires a Herculean amount of strength. It requires going against a deeply primal part of our minds that believes our very existence will be threatened by leaving the safety of that little society. It quite literally feels like a life or death decision. In religious or spiritual groups, not just our lives, but the fate of our souls, may seem to lie in the balance. The enormity and the bravery of this decision to walk away from the controlling confines of these groups cannot be overstated.

While getting out is a great act of liberation, it can also be intensely painful to lose the sense of community and the deep connections that we experienced within the group, despite their problematic nature. Since high-control relationships and groups foster an unhealthy amount of dependency that is sold as "community," those of us emerging from these worlds often face intense emotional loss from the thing that so often drew us into that world in the first place: a sense of belonging and a need for connection. High control groups are full of hardworking, intelligent, compassionate individuals who are seeking deep meaningful connections and sense of purpose. These are the types of individuals who are targeted by narcissistic leaders (or partners) because they have skills, traits and assets to contribute to that group's mission or simply to the leader him/herself. Lazy, unintelligent, unmotivated and/or ungiving individuals are less likely to be targeted because they have little value to offer the leader. Therefore, these groups are commonly filled with big-hearted and idealistic souls who are eager to connect with one another. Unhealthy or not, for better or worse, we knew how that system operated and we "belonged" within it. Getting out most often involves leaving each of these former connections and comrades behind, only to face a cold world outside of the safety of the group, completely alone.

The "us" versus "them" mentality is one of the defining characteristics of culty groups of any and all kinds. The practice of shunning is a common tactic used in cultic and high-control groups, as a result. Sometimes shunning is an official policy built into the structure of the group and other times it is simply a by-product of stepping away, thereby leaving the "us" and becoming a "them" by default. No matter the cause, the experience of being ostracized, ignored, excluded, given the silent treatment and/or shunned is brutally painful. Studies have shown that it lights up the same centers of the brain as physical pain.

A *Psychology Today* article explains:

> *Humans have a primal need for social support. Without a sense of belonging—a feeling of emotional safety and context—people come to fear that their very lives are at risk. They lose the ability to trust and connect with others, instead becoming consumed by the task of surviving alone. Shunning, therefore, is like a social death penalty—and studies prove this point. Exclusion has been found to cause pain that cuts deeper and lasts longer than a physical injury, according to Dr. Kipling D. Williams, a distinguished professor of psychological sciences at Purdue University who is noted for his unique studies of ostracism (https://www.psychologytoday.com/us/blog/brothers-sisters-strangers/202403/how-religious-shunning-ruins-lives).*

Many survivors will know this pain very well, having experienced it as a consequence of leaving their groups. In my experience, the pain of shunning was a fundamental and recurring trauma, a tactic routinely employed by our leader within the group to punish, control and manipulate. I can personally attest to the physical pain it causes as well as the consequence of "becoming consumed by the task of surviving alone" in the face of this intensely painful form of emotional abuse. The damage done by the experience of being shunned, depending on the intensity, severity and duration, is one of the challenges we are faced with in our healing in order to learn to trust and connect with others once again.

Despite my considerable fortune in retaining three close connections from my former group, as we each embarked on our own new paths, we each faced our futures by ourselves. When I got out, I reached out to a few former friends to let them know I was free. I had a fiercely supportive sister and two friends from my life before the cult who eagerly welcomed me back. In the months that followed, I rallied the courage to reach out to a couple more folks who had been close to me in my previous life. Unfortunately, the damage I'd done to those relationships when I'd severed them was too great. They did not respond at all.

There are many losses that you simply cannot recover after time spent in a high control group, and those pertaining to lost relationships may be one of the worst. *Time* lost, overall, tends to be the most intense grief from which survivors suffer, in my experience. For me, the loss of so many years of my life to high-control is a grief which I may never fully wrap my mind around, and the loss of the relationships I had—or could have had—is a close second.

After a decade of uncommonly close relationships in the group—relationships with little or no healthy boundaries and some involving a great deal of forced camaraderie—I had no close-knit community around me. I found myself approaching mid-life and starting over from scratch in every way. *Everything* was new, even the handful of old relationships I was lucky enough to recover. I was a different person now and they were too. There was no familiarity in any part of my life, no foundation stone to which I might tether myself. I felt intensely alone.

The need to connect with others and to have a place of belonging in the world is primal. That primal need is one of the most effective means cult leaders and other narcissistic abusers use to manipulate their prey into complying with them. In more primitive times, having a place within the group was essential to survival. Being banished, or otherwise ending up out on your own, outside the safety of the village, would likely result in death. Safety meant staying within the group, which required behaving within the accepted norms of the group and fulfilling the group's expectations and demands.

When we struggle to understand why our cultic or narcissistic captors had so much power over us—or when others struggle to understand this about us—it is because we are drastically underestimating the power of this primal programming within the human psyche. The community, and thereby "protection," afforded us by staying within the confines of our high-control situation is truly captivating. To risk losing it feels like a life or death choice on a physical, emotional and psychological level. Sometimes, it literally is. It is the very same power that keeps individuals locked into toxic family dynamics, although that scenario tends to be a more socially acceptable version of cultic control.

When you begin to conceive of the power of this primal need within the human psyche, it will give you a whole new level of appreciation for the radical bravery and profound strength you successfully summoned to not only get out, but to *stay out* of a trauma-inducing, high-control situation. Once we are out, however, we may struggle to feel safe again, both outside of our former group and also in proximity to any other potential groups of people. It can be difficult to determine safe interpersonal dynamics from unhealthy ones. Nonetheless, that basic human need for connection has not disappeared. Recognizing and understanding this need is a critical first step. Finding healthy, safe opportunities to fulfill that need is the essential next step.

Connection after Disconnection

Opening ourselves up to connection when we are coping with and recovering from C-PTSD can be overwhelming, intimidating and downright terrifying. Complex PTSD is characterized as relational trauma. It is commonly the result of trauma incurred over prolonged periods of abuse by someone who is close to us and often in a position of authority over us. It may be a parent, significant other, spouse, employer, therapist, religious or spiritual leader, doctor, kidnapper, cult leader, or any combination of these. Regardless of the specific circumstances, C-PTSD does serious relational damage. While it is human to feel some trepidation when opening yourself up to the world and making yourself vulnerable to other people, it may feel impossibly frightening to those suffering with C-PTSD.

At the same time, learning to build safe, healthy connections with others can be the ultimate antidote to C-PTSD. It is the very thing we crave, that we need and the avenue by which we were hurt most deeply. In turn, it can also be our salvation. It is time to summon those vast stores of courage within yourself once more—yes, *once again,* warrior.

Unlike the forced insta-bond that so often draws us into high-control relationships due to love bombing and the rapid dissolution of healthy boundaries, building deep connections takes time. It takes effort and repetition. It requires us to put ourselves out into the world and to invite others back into our heavily guarded worlds. However, we can forge these connections incrementally and in safe ways. We don't have to open ourselves completely or too fast. We can start by tiptoeing out into the community around us and finding opportunities to be around other human beings.

Within the confines of my group, I was always on guard for doing or saying the wrong thing that might land me in hot water. Usually, this was unavoidable as the leader's moods were volatile and unpredictable. Even though my intuitive senses assisted enormously in navigating this environment, it is unavoidable that when you live in close proximity with someone who defaults to anger, criticism and punitive shunning behaviors, you will be subjected to these influences. Like others in close proximity, I was subjected to them *all the time.* With very little connection, and no meaningful relationships, outside of this dynamic, the entire world comes to feel hard, angry, scary, mean and unsafe. I could not consciously realize, while I was in it, that this perspective had completely overtaken my reality. Nor could I fully realize that life did not have to be that way—indeed, it was not that way for others.

In a critically defining moment during my last months within the group, when I was already questioning the confines of my microscopic little world and how I ended up there, I took the unprecedented opportunity to spend two days away from the group and the leader. Understand, this action was unheard of and was only made possible by my deep and growing realization that I could not go on living the way that I was. In the months leading up to this, I bravely dared to forge a reconnection with my sister who had never stopped making occasional attempts to reach me over the many years of our estrangement. During this two-day reprieve, I went to visit her for the first time in over a decade and I was astounded by what I observed.

There was a harmony within her home the likes of which I had completely forgotten existed. When she made a mistake by leaving her wallet at home in a rushed, last-minute trip to the store and had to double back to retrieve it, throwing off the timeline for our dinner plans, she was not criticized, yelled at or berated by her husband. Instead, he assisted her. It was as if it were no big deal at all. Most importantly, I noted that *she was not afraid.* She did not fear the repercussions of making a human mistake. She was not going to be punished, the night would not be ruined, and she would not have to endure a lecture about her "unawareness" and the paucity of her spiritual growth because she made a mistake or exhibited forgetfulness. She would not be harshly admonished and bullied into doing worksheets to correct her wayward mind. I, on the other hand, was never *not* afraid.

I was truly stunned by the interactions I observed over those two days. The disparity between everyday life in this household and in mine could not have been more stark. I had completely forgotten that people existed within homes that were not ruled by fear, anxiety and paranoia. Perhaps I never knew it to begin with. I struggled to trust it. I kept waiting for the other shoe to drop. I questioned my sister, as casually as I could, on our second trip back to the store: Is this normal? Is your husband putting on an act because there's company present? What is your relationship really like? I could tell by her response to my questions that not only was the dynamic of partnership and equality very normal in her relationship, but my skepticism and shock about it was a little less than normal.

Those two days presented a realization from which, ultimately, I could not turn back. Other people did not live the way that I did. More importantly, maybe there was another life possible *for me,* one with a little more kindness, a little more gentleness, a little more equality, a little more freedom. Maybe the way I was living was not only not normal, but maybe, just maybe, it was not actually *right* after all. It certainly did not feel right. The safety of my sister's home environment was so utterly foreign to me that a small part of my mind recognized that my version of "normal" was perhaps very, very wrong.

A couple of months later, when I was free and beginning to venture back out into the world at large, I was continually dismayed to discover that, for the most part, people were *kind.* People were warm. People were welcoming. People were considerate. People were respectful. People were friendly. "People"—wherever I encountered them—shocked me over and over again with their everyday courtesy and gentleness. Perhaps the world was not in as bad a shape as I'd been compelled to believe over these years of cultic indoctrination. Or perhaps the world *is* in pretty bad shape, but even so, it is not nearly as hard, scary, threatening and angry as life under narcissistic abuse is on a moment-to-moment basis. To my dismay, I have come to learn that, overall, *people* are mostly *good.*

Finding Connection Now

How do we begin to test the waters of human connection again? As with all aspects of recovery, the answer will be unique to each person, but once again, I will endeavor to provide a jumping-off point. The first step is to intend to connect with the outside world. The next step is to seek opportunities. The third step is to jump on those opportunities when you find them!

Making a connection can be as simple as engaging with the barista at the coffee counter. In fact, cafes and coffee shops are great places to take yourself for some basic human interaction. Whether you take a good book, do some work on a laptop or just scroll on your phone, making an effort to put yourself in communal environments is an excellent first step. Make sure to look up and around you once in a while and maybe try leaving the earbuds at home, as these will often deter a potential interaction before it can occur.

I worked as a barista for many years before I met the life coach. What I loved most about my work was the communal aspect. Seeing my "regulars" and routinely meeting new people through my job cultivated an enormous sense of community for me. Although I no longer work as a barista, I still gravitate toward the coffee shop and cafe environment for the same purpose. If you find a place where you might become a frequent visitor, the opportunities for connection can be amplified. In the early days of recovery, these simple and limited interactions are often enough. They are comfortably safe and light enough to be not-too-draining, and yet, they can provide a sense of connection and belonging within the world at large.

As your capacity for engagement expands, try looking for meet up groups or activities in areas of interest for you. Check out community boards in your local coffee shops, gym or library for upcoming events and activities. Search online for these opportunities as well.

Maybe your green thumb is hankering to get in the dirt and there's a community garden you can become involved in. Perhaps there's some hiking, biking or sightseeing to be done in your area that piques your interest. If so, chances are high that there is a group available to the public dedicated to doing exactly that. Love reading? There is a movement of meet-ups for readers where individuals can gather at a specific time and place to silently and independently read.

Afterwards, there is opportunity to come together and share with one another about your books—participation strictly optional. Search for a #silentbookclub in your area. Love the culinary arts? Find a cooking class to take. Looking for an excuse to get outside and run around? Join a community kickball league. Many cities and towns offer a variety of adult community sports groups, from soccer and softball to bowling and corn hole.

Any form of expression or creativity is freeing and healing for our spirit. Creative pursuits are an excellent way to till the soil of our true selves and reconnect us to our innermost being. These can absolutely be done in the privacy of your own home and I encourage you to do so. However, they may also offer a springboard for connection as well. Taking an art class or joining a writing group may be an excellent avenue to explore. You may research to see if there is a community arts center near you with opportunities such as these. The structured nature of these various activities provides an opportunity to experience positive, healing interactions which help to foster a sense of belonging within the world around you, while remaining brief and safe enough to allow sufficient space for us to connect only to the extent we feel comfortable at any given point.

Personal ads aren't just for romantic connections anymore. Just as dating apps replaced the personals section of the newspaper, there are now apps for finding and making new friends. You could find your new BFF through a friend finding app! This modality allows you to "meet" and connect with others through a virtual platform, allowing you to build some rapport and ensure that you feel comfortable with your new acquaintance before meeting up in person. For some of us, the virtual platform may be enough, to start with.

In a world that has become rapidly isolated due to pandemics, remote working and social media, cult and narcissistic abuse survivors are not the only ones seeking and desperately missing genuine human interaction. This isolation has become a plague to us all as a society. As a result, opportunities are rapidly growing to use technology for finding and connecting with others over any possible interest. We can use these resources to find levels of connection that feel safe and appealing to us.

The happy news is that the more actively you pursue your own interests, the greater your chances of connecting with others who have similar interests. Yes, this does require getting off the couch, walking out of your front door and entering the wild of the public. You get to take this at your own pace and engage to whatever degree feels comfortable for you.

Making new friends and building relationships takes time for a variety of reasons. For one, time is required to organically learn about others, build trust, and gradually share more and more of yourself as you deem that it is safe to do so. There is no magic formula for this process that I am aware of, unfortunately. It will be unique to each individual situation. It is normal, and perhaps even wise, to be wary of groups of any kind when we escape high control situations. Culty aspects exist among countless businesses, community organizations, political groups, spiritual or religious groups, exercise programs and almost every sector of society, as it turns out, to varying degrees. In addition, narcissistic individuals are not limited to these groups. We can naturally become phobic of organized groups as a result of our experiences, not to mention distrustful of others in general. Once again, I have found that the best way to ensure our own safety is by nurturing our relationship with ourselves *first* and continually.

On top of that, recovery is exhausting. There's just no other way to put it. Our capacity to engage with the world at large can be extremely limited in these early days, as our bodies, minds and hearts slowly mend. This reality is yet another reason for taking time to slowly build new, safe relationships around us.

For all these reasons, I have learned that it is important to be patient in the process of finding and building new relationships. In three years, I have managed to establish a single handful of new relationships which are still gradually evolving into deeper, closer, trusted friends. I found out that it is difficult for *any* adult to form new relationships as our lives usually lack the commonalities that assisted with forming those quick bonds earlier in life, such as those friends we found during the developmental stages of going to school, playing sports, communal dormitory living and/or just stepping out into the world on our own. Survivors of abuse, however, have the additional task of overcoming deeply held fears and doubts about allowing others near us and our inner worlds. We can be skeptical, distrustful and prickly when it comes to strangers entering our personal space. That is why taking the time to rebuild our internal connection with ourselves is so crucial to the success of any new relationships we discover, and that, once again, takes *time*.

We talked about the role of support groups as an educational tool in trauma recovery. I want to acknowledge that these are obvious opportunities for connection as well. However, support group connections tend to be different from the ones you are building fresh out in the wild world. We tend to share much more personal information about ourselves much earlier in this environment, specifically pertaining to the theme of that support group, than we may with the barista at our local coffee shop. Support groups come with a built-in sense of camaraderie and the bond of shared trauma, or at least the understanding of such. While boundaries and flood prevention are still important to have in a support group atmosphere, this should be a safe space where such occurrences can be easily mitigated and understood.

Want to double down on recovery practice goodness? Here's a suggestion that combines opportunities-to-connect with extending-care-toward-others: Go volunteer! What better way to gently forge your path out into the world than finding an activity that has extra meaning for you? Help yourself while helping others. Find volunteer opportunities that speak to you, and go serve your community while also meeting others and building new connections. Food pantries, soup kitchens, men's and women's shelters, crisis centers, community gardens, library initiatives and animal shelters are just a small selection of groups and organizations that can almost always use an extra hand.

Speaking of animal shelters, I have one last word to offer on the topic of connection. We touched on it in Chapter 7: Nature and Nutrition, but it bears repeating here. Relational trauma presents unique challenges for building relationships and learning to trust people again. Animals, and pets in particular, can be a huge asset in this process. I've seen trauma survivors who have experienced profoundly healing effects from reciprocal, loving relationships with pets. Our pets have a natural instinct for aligning with us emotionally and mentally without the use of a shared verbal language. We share a more instinctual and empathic relationship with animals which can be easier than that which we share with other humans. The bottomless well of love that they have to give, as well as the love that they are capable of receiving from us as we care for them, should not be minimized. For many of us, connecting with an animal may be the precursor to attempting to connect with other humans, and that is more than okay. Connecting with animals counts too, and that connection can be transformative. In addition, the emotional support that our animals provide can be lifesaving for those of us struggling with depression, anxiety and the host of other emotional issues resulting from trauma.

It is vitally important that we be gentle, compassionate and kind with ourselves in this process. Most importantly, we must *listen* to our hearts and our minds as we undertake to open ourselves back up to meaningful connection. This is the point in which it is so vital that we have learned to tune into our intuition and discern its signals, for that is the most powerful protection we have in the valiant process of opening ourselves back up to connection. Give yourself grace, give yourself patience and honor whatever comes up for you in this process. If something feels unsafe, take a step back. If it feels like too much, slow down. This is *your* journey and you are the captain of it. Do what feels best for *you.*

Romantic Relationships: A Word of Caution

Building a rapport of friendly interactions with other human beings is a great goal and a huge stride in the right direction. However, I am aware that romance is often one of the first ideas that pops up on the topic of "connection," and that it can present a great challenge to the newly free who are not already in a committed relationship. To that end, I would offer a word of caution.

In addiction recovery, the newly sober are warned away from engaging in new romantic entanglements within the first year of recovery. This rule of thumb is a safe bet for those in their first year of recovery from high-control and abusive relationships, as well. There are many reasons for this, not least of which is the time and space needed to prioritize your healing and do the work of rebuilding your relationship *with yourself.* This self-work will play a critical role in the success of our future relationships. Intimate relationships require enormous work and attention. When we begin to pour ourselves into those connections before reaching a critical mass of reconnection within ourselves, we are most likely to fall out of balance and it becomes all too easy to lose our way.

There are countless tales of those who escaped their abusive environments with the assistance of a new romantic connection or who found a new love immediately afterward. Again, each path is unique and you must do what is right and best *for you.* I do not pass judgment on these situations because I do believe that (safe and healthy) new relationships have the potential to offer an enormous amount of healing. The key here is "safe and healthy," which is less likely to occur at this early stage of trauma recovery. Conversely, I do not believe anyone has suffered harm further down the road for having taken the time to build their relationship with themselves *first.* Successful and healthy relationships born out of the earliest stages of recovery, or the point of escaping abuse, while possible, seem to be more of an exception than a rule.

Nine months after I got out, I found myself building a connection with a man to whom I felt a deep attraction. I was hesitant to proceed because I held that one-year-rule for myself. While that early connection was broken off before a relationship ensued, I did come back to that connection at the one-year anniversary of my great escape from cultic control. At that point, I chose to commit myself to a relationship with that man. Even though I was a full year into my recovery, I discovered that it was still incredibly early to attempt a relationship on that level. I learned a lot of lessons from the experience, not least of which was the importance of prioritizing my reconnection with myself over an intimate, romantic connection. Another year later, much of my healing work would reset as I navigated the triggers and the loss that early relationship caused.

After living in an emotional desert for so very long, and then finally escaping the brutal atmosphere of my high-control group, my heart and soul positively yearned for the life-giving affection and emotional nourishment that early relationship promised. I know well the deep pull such a relationship can have. At the same time, I also know the deep aversion we may feel to any attachment at all after our abusive experiences. In both instances, self-love and inner reconnection are the true remedy.

Your tendency toward, or away, from romantic connections will be unique to you. Your timeline for when you can, or desire to, safely engage in a new relationship is also completely up to you. In the earliest days of recovery, however, I would caution you to take your time, move slowly and deeply reconsider any new romantic or emotional attachments. We are yet so vulnerable and tender at this stage and just navigating day-to-day life can drain what energetic reserves we have. We are just beginning to unpack and understand our own trauma, let alone share that burden with someone else who may not have the slightest inkling of what to do with it or how to support you in it. In the worst of possible outcomes, we may actually end up in the hands of someone who seems externally different but offers what turns out to be a familiar emotional landscape to that which we have just so bravely left.

My natural tendency, after a lifetime of trying to be good enough, has been to pour myself into others. The closer they are to me, the more I pour. In my new relationship, I easily lost my balance, and at times, my recovery process and health suffered to the degree that I gave away more than I had to give when I still needed so much time and attention for myself. While that relationship offered me enormous insights into my growth and healing, for which I am grateful, it also caused an enormous amount of upheaval and pain from which I then also had to recover. Too many times, I put my own needs on the back burner to serve the needs of the relationship and the other person. This was a consequence of not having a solid-enough foundation rebuilt within myself to successfully discern my own needs and to stand on business when they were not met.

If there were a Ninja Warrior Challenge for practicing self-love, it would be romantic relationships. Although these relationships seem to provide the very things we are so desperately needing, it is the very fact that we are so desperately needing them that is most likely to doom those relationships. It is not fair to throw ourselves into a Ninja Warrior Challenge without having completed the proper training to perform on that level. In the meantime, wrap your arms around yourself, give yourself a huge hug and remind yourself how precious, lovable and beautiful you are. Give yourself the affection, encouragement, quality time, words of affirmation, gifts, acts of service and expressions of love that you deserve. *Love yourself.*

While we are still desperately looking to others to have something fulfilled within us, it is unlikely that we will attract the truly healthy, balanced and loving relationships into our lives that will actually feed and support us. It is human nature to desire to connect with others deeply, personally and romantically. Until we have made some steady progress in the art of fulfilling our own desperate needs and wants, however, our romantic relationships will meet us on the level of *desperate* needing and wanting. The trick is to be honest with ourselves about where we are in that process. I have noticed that most of us are loath to admit that we have this tendency within us, especially women. It is not considered posh in modern western culture, so we tend to disclaim it within ourselves. Therefore, we must summon the courage to look at ourselves truthfully, unrelentingly and to be brutally honest about our needs, our wants, our desires and our motivations. We don't have to tell them to anyone else. But we *must* have the courage to admit them to ourselves.

If you're unsure where you stand on this, here is one barometer that you may use. The degree to which you struggle *not* to engage in romantic dalliances is a strong indicator of the degree to which you feel a void within yourself that you do not yet know how to fill on your own. It is to a similar degree that you are likely to attract partners who are equipped, or *not* equipped, to engage in a healthy, truly loving, safe and reciprocal relationship with you. This is where we return, once again, to the deep and difficult work of sitting with ourselves, listening to ourselves, feeling into our lonely spaces, and ultimately, learning to be the greatest lover of ourselves that there ever was or will ever be.

Others of us, though, may tend more toward the loner or reclusive persuasion. This is a protective mechanism which may also be adopted in the wake of abusive relationships and one toward which I have at times swayed, as well. After enduring immense relational hardships, it can be extremely appealing to simply withdraw from the world and spare yourself the risk that comes with human connections. It is true that relationships of all kinds require effort, attention and energy from us. It is true that opening ourselves to other human beings puts us at risk of being hurt sometimes, much like opening our front doors and walking out into the world puts us at risk of catching a virus from time to time. Yet if we don't ever leave our homes, we will miss out on all the beauty, adventure, experiences and *life* that is waiting out there to be lived, tasted and felt. Relationships are one of our greatest catalysts for personal growth and fulfillment. To forego them altogether, albeit an option, is a choice to forego a great deal of what life has to offer.

Through this journey, I have come to view myself as my own fiercest protector, and I see protecting myself as my solemn duty. It is up to me to vet the people, places and situations I allow into my life. It is up to me to protect my emotional, physical and mental well-being. It is up to me to protect my heart and provide it with the love and care it requires. It is up to me to safeguard my life, not only from predators, but all those who would take from me and not feed me reciprocally. It is up to me to ensure that all those who have access to me match my give, whether that be friend, romantic interest, coworker or family member.

Having said all of that, don't get it twisted! I am a huge fan of strong, healthy, safe relationships—of all kinds. I believe that each of us deserve to have loving, genuine and equal partnerships. I believe that genuine love (in every form) is the greatest cure, the greatest aspiration and the greatest achievement that one can have in life. I also believe that we too often settle for that which may resemble love to us, based on the media we consume, instead of reaching for the real thing, quite often because we don't know what the real thing looks or feels like. It is our duty to discover and provide the real thing for ourselves, within ourselves. If we access that first, we will have the real thing within us to give to another when that safe, healthy other comes along.

10

The F Word: The Secret Sauce of Self Love

Forgiveness can be a sensitive topic. It is one of the most radical and transformative healing practices in which we can engage. However, the very idea of forgiveness can be intensely triggering. I find that it is an important part of healing because complex trauma survivors are often racked with self-blame by a loud, relentless inner critic. If the connection between these ideas is not immediately obvious, stick with me into a deeper dive of this tool.

Usually when we talk about forgiveness, the act is directed toward someone who has hurt us. Often, forgiveness is mistaken for being an act of absolution in which the wrongdoer is relieved of their guilt by the one who has been hurt. This idea can be downright insulting to someone who has been horribly abused. I do not personally subscribe to this definition of forgiveness.

I believe that forgiveness is a process in which we gain a new perspective and in which we are freed from the burden of pain which we carry.

It is not a condoning of another's deeds. It is not a self-righteous act in which we bestow unwarranted mercy on those who have done us wrong, making us the bigger and better person. It is not a set of empty words that we spew in order to "move on" or "move past" a painful incident. I also do not believe that forgiveness equates to reconciliation. Even if someone does choose to forgive an abuser, that does not mean that they should be expected to resume a relationship with a toxic or dangerous person.

Forgiveness is a strictly internal process in which we suspend our judgments, interpretations and beliefs in order to allow fresh, healing energies to flow through our minds and hearts, bestowing renewal and healing *on us*. It is not something we do for another. It is something we do for ourselves. In some cases, it may be done in a moment; often, it is a process which unfolds over time.

The choice to forgive or not forgive an abuser is an intensely personal one. I cannot tell anyone else what is right for them when it comes to forgiving a person who has willfully caused them great harm. It is a question which we all must face within ourselves and come to our own conclusions in our own due time.

What I *can* tell you is that the power of forgiveness is great in setting us free from our pain and our suffering. Although we tend to focus on others when it comes to the act of forgiveness, there is more to the story. One of the most powerful applications of this healing tool comes when we direct it toward *ourselves*.

I know…the thought of forgiving ourselves presents its own challenges and it may even elicit greater disdain than the idea of forgiving an abuser. If so, I just want to say, I get it. Please hang in there with me and take this opportunity to investigate.

For some, the idea of forgiving yourself may seem preposterous. "What do I have to forgive myself for? After all, I'm the victim here! Victim's rights dictate my innocence. I'm good! No need for self-forgiveness here" (crosses arms, *hmph*). This perspective would be a natural reaction stemming from the idea that forgiveness is about letting someone off the hook for a wrongdoing. Since that is not my interpretation of forgiveness, that perspective does not apply to what I am posing here.

For others, the idea of self-forgiveness may immediately cause your guts to churn. You may feel uncomfortable, self-conscious, or just want to run away from this idea. Your inborn sense of guilt may be so strong that you prefer not to look in that direction at all. It may come just a little too close to thoughts and feelings you'd rather not entertain.

I've saved the best for last because I am aware of how many unpleasant and uncomfortable reactions this idea can trigger. Oftentimes, we find the greatest growth and healing rewards hidden behind where our greatest fear and resistance lies. If that's you, just take a moment to recognize that there may be great benefits for you to reap if you should choose to do the scary, dirty work of excavating what lies here for you.

Regardless of your reaction, I believe that most of us suffering from C-PTSD have work to do in forgiving ourselves. The circumstances that lead to C-PTSD also foster shame, self-blame and guilt. Even though we may not have done anything wrong at all, we typically blame ourselves anyway. Usually, this internal guilt-and-self-blame factory has been cultivated in us by our abusers through a variety of techniques, including blaming, outright yelling, belittling, berating, gaslighting and accusing. In cases of religious abuse, the concept of

God is often used to condemn us, as well.

You will never meet a greater victim than a genuine narcissist and so those of us in close relationship with them will have often been painted as the abuser and victimizer *by* the narcissist. Since the narcissist's victims are typically sensitive and empathic people, the victims tend to take these accusations on, blaming, doubting and second-guessing themselves long before they ever hold the narcissist accountable for his or her own behavior. By the time we've developed C-PTSD, all of this guilt and blame has usually been deeply internalized. It is the source of a great deal of our sufferings, our self-doubt and our struggle to connect with others.

As a result, learning to forgive ourselves—that is, to see and embrace our inherent innocence and worth—is a key component of not only rebuilding a healthy relationship with ourselves, but coming to truly love ourselves. Self-forgiveness is equal to self-love. Whether you choose to extend forgiveness to anyone else or not, please practice forgiving yourself first and foremost. *You* deserve it more than anything.

So, What Is Forgiveness?

Back in 2006, when I was googling "how to be happy" and discovered that gratitude was the key, I continued to encounter one other concept over and over again as an equal cornerstone for happiness. That concept was forgiveness. While I lay on my bed racking my brain for a source of gratitude, I bristled entirely at the idea of forgiveness. It wasn't that I didn't think I needed to forgive. I absolutely knew that lack of forgiveness was a major source of my discontent. It made sense.

The problem was that it overwhelmed me. I had no idea how to actually *do* it. Despite my research, I could not find any clear explanation or practical steps for how to do it, either.

Today, when you delve into the topic of forgiveness, similar messages arise. We are told that forgiving means "choosing to let go" and "deciding to release our anger and hurt." Yes, but *how*? The answers I encountered utterly frustrated me. They were beautiful ideas, but they offered no practical steps for application. After all, how does one simply decide to no longer be hurt, angry or devastated after experiences of abuse, a whole childhood marked by traumatic experiences, or even a singular, painful incident?

In 2008, during my first year of weekly sessions with the life coach, I was offered a new definition and practical steps for practicing forgiveness. Finally! For the first time in my life, someone offered me a tangible, step-by-step system for implementing and practicing forgiveness that did not reduce it to high minded, ethereal platitudes. In many ways, I believe it was the concrete answer to this single question, "How do I forgive?", that had the most impact in winning my allegiance to this new spiritual path and to the life coach as my self-ordained "teacher."

I learned that forgiveness need not be reserved only for those who have hurt us, but that it can be used for literally *any* person, place, or thing that causes us distress in any way. The purpose of forgiveness is to restore our minds and hearts to a state of peace. This perspective was brand new to me and it is why the concept of forgiveness became so fundamental to our everyday lives. Forgiveness became the antidote to every problem and every source of pain that we experienced.

It is natural, when emerging from these systems of control, to want to throw out all things related to the group, both in terms of concepts and practices as well as physical limitations imposed by that system. However, there are usually some nuggets of wisdom, truth or light within that space which drew us into them to begin with. For survivors of cultic control, we must face the challenge of sorting out truth from lies, meaning from indoctrination, and that which offers us value from that which was simply used to control. For me, one of the nuggets of truth and value that I have extracted from my early days of study was learning a definition for forgiveness that made sense to me and a practical method for implementing that definition.

It can be a confusing and arduous process to sort out what we truly think, feel, and believe after we have been indoctrinated by a particular belief system or set of practices. While I will likely spend many years to come working through that process, I decided early on in my recovery journey that I would not throw out the baby with the bathwater, so to speak. My leader had no authorship of any of the ideas, concepts or techniques that I was introduced to in his office. He was merely a middle man and an opportunist. To throw away every piece of value I received through my own personal development work and self-study would be to cede any and every hard-earned benefit I gained during those fourteen years to the very person who manipulated and abused me with them. I choose not to give him that power or that pleasure any longer. I have chosen to retain only that which works for me, serves me, and assists me in my ongoing healing journey.

To that end, I have found that forgiveness does, indeed, offer me great opportunities for healing. I can also confirm that it does require a simple, internal decision to "let go" just like all those online sources stated when I first began researching the process. Forgiveness is one of the oldest and most fundamental concepts found in healing, personal growth and spiritual studies of all kinds. I continue to employ the basic tenets and general method of forgiveness I learned because I experience great benefit from it. However, I no longer engage in the "forgiveness worksheets" we were compelled to do on a daily basis in our group as a form of self-flagellation, rather I turn to forgiveness only when and where I feel ready to do so. In many ways, the process laid out within the chapters of this book is a living, breathing process of self-forgiveness, both internal and external. After all, forgiveness and healing go hand in hand.

Because I have witnessed these steps of forgiveness offering benefit to many others outside of our little group as well, I will offer them to you here so that you may try them for yourself, if you desire. I will first provide an explanation of the process, followed by a condensed list of the steps for easy reference. I have come across a number of forgiveness worksheet methods from a wide variety of sources which offer similar processes for implementing this practice, so this technique cannot be credited to any one person or philosophy. You may find it helpful in navigating your own internal process of forgiveness, if and when you should choose to engage it. Like every other idea and suggestion in this book, I encourage you to simply take and use whatever is helpful to you.

The Forgiveness Process

Practicing forgiveness is a conscious, intentional act. While it can be done in a single moment once we are truly ready to make the shift, we can also escort ourselves through that shift with this practice. In order to do so, I recommend setting aside a block of uninterrupted time where you can sit down and focus on mentally and emotionally moving through this process. Pen and paper will be the most effective means of working through the steps, especially at the beginning. Breath should be your steady companion throughout this process. Remember to breath before, during, and after each step in order to facilitate the processing and releasing of the upsetting thoughts and feelings.

The first step of the forgiveness process is to write down a brief description of the person, place, thing or situation which has upset you. (Remember that you can use this technique to help you process and move through any source of pain, upset or grief in your life—not just people who have hurt or upset you.) Then, list each of the feelings that were evoked by this situation, person, place, or thing. For each of the feelings you listed, write down the thought(s) in your mind behind that feeling. Lastly—and this requires a bit of brutal honesty with ourselves—write down the way in which you wish to punish the person, place, or thing that has caused you harm. This identifies our human desire for revenge, to right the scales of justice, and/or to protect ourselves from further harm.

Now, take a moment to go back through these lists with intention. For each feeling listed, allow yourself just a moment to truly *feel* it, as we discussed in the section about feeling our feelings. No judgment here. After giving yourself that moment to feel, affirm to yourself that you are now choosing to release this feeling in order that you may feel better. Move on to your list of thoughts and do the same thing. Review each thought and then affirm to yourself that you are choosing to release this thought/belief so that you may feel better. Finally, take a moment to review the ways in which you desire to exact punishment and make the conscious, willing decision to release your need to punish this person, place, or thing.

These moments of affirmation are the literal application of that concept we so often hear which states that forgiveness is about "letting go" and "moving on." The difference is that we are not sweeping the feelings and the issues under the rug. We are looking at them, embracing them and then making a conscious choice to release them *in order that* a new, fresh and positive perspective may be introduced into our minds and hearts in their place. The process of releasing opens up space within us for something else to replace our painful perspectives. It doesn't invalidate our experience, rather it allows us to replace the painful effects of our experience with some peace and possibly even some new revelations about both ourselves and others. Without this space for fresh perspectives, possibilities and opportunities, we stay stuck in the same mental and emotional ruts. Since our perceptions dictate our experience of reality, this tool can be used to exert more conscious control over the way we experience our lives. That is the power of forgiveness and that is why it is done for *ourselves,* first and foremost. Yes, it provides additional benefits to the entire world around us, but that is just icing on the cake.

The next step is twofold. It is to identify one truly loving thought about the person, place or thing you are forgiving and write it down. Focus on *feeling* that loving thought in your heart. You also want to identify and write down one truly loving thought about *yourself,* and genuinely feel that thought in your heart as well. Finding a point of love or appreciation for the subject of your forgiveness work can sometimes be a stumper, but choosing to focus on this aspect and allowing that feeling to replace the former grievance is the critical component to cementing the forgiveness practice. In the same way, finding and affirming a loving thought about yourself in each of these practices is an equally critical component.

This step of the process is important because it rests on the foundational premise that what we offer to others, we offer to ourselves—and vice versa. Whether it is conscious or not, we cannot hold blame, judgment and anger for another without experiencing the pain of blame, judgment, and anger within our own hearts, minds, and bodies. We know we are truly willing to forgive once we are able to complete this step of the process.

That brings us to the final stage. Take a moment now to reflect on your original goal for this person, place or thing. What is it that you wanted from them or it? Think about this in terms of the positive outcome, goal, or agenda you held that was not met and write this down. For example, instead of saying "I want them to *stop* doing x,y,z," state what you *do* want from them, instead.

Getting clear on this goal helps us to recognize the underlying source of our pain or grief. Our unmet needs, dashed hopes and treasured goals for people, places, and things outside of ourselves lies at the heart of the pain and turmoil that forgiveness can free us from. Just as we did in the beginning with our painful thoughts and feelings, we now affirm that we are willing and choosing to release and let go of this goal we have been holding, sometimes unconsciously. Releasing this goal frees us because, at the end of the day, we only have control over our *own* choices, behaviors, thoughts, feelings, and actions. Once I have reached that internal state of letting go, I like to draw a line through the goal that I originally wrote down, signifying my decision to cancel it. It is at this point that we affirm our own power to choose how we think, feel, and respond to every person, place, and thing in our lives.

Finally, take a moment to express gratitude to yourself for the work you have done here. Also, take a moment to recognize how you feel now, upon completion of the process, and make a note of your current inner state at this point.

You may find it helpful to keep a notebook or journal for this practice and to date your entries. It can be interesting to look back at them at a later time and see how your feelings, perspectives, and life have evolved since you did this work. And remember that forgiveness is a process, one which we may have to repeat many times for the seemingly same issue, person, or situation as we traverse our healing journey, each time reaching a new layer of healing.

The process I have laid out here does take practice. It may feel awkward, foreign or laborious at first. As with any new skill, it takes time and repetition to develop proficiency and you will find that it becomes easier, faster, and more natural the more frequently you engage in it. For me, the most consistent outcome I experience from my forgiveness practice is a sense of relief. My body feels calmer and more grounded. My head feels clearer. Anxiety and tension release. It is for these effects that I return to this process when I need it.

Perhaps most critically of all, these steps can be used to forgive and heal our anger and judgments *toward ourselves*. You do this by making yourself the object of the forgiveness process and thinking of yourself in the third person as you go through the practice. I cannot tell you how many worksheets I completed on Christina, listing my feelings and thoughts about her, my judgments, my goals, and my agendas, and choosing to let each of those go. It is for this purpose, above all, that I offer these steps to you as another tool in your self-forgiveness healing journey.

Steps to Forgiveness

Breathe between each step

1. Identify the person, place, or thing that is upsetting you and briefly describe the reason for your distress. (*Issue: "My Job", Description: I am upset because I got passed over for the big promotion that I thought I was going to get.)*
2. List all of the resulting feelings you are experiencing (*anger, hurt, fear, frustration, anxiety, etc.*).
3. List each of the corresponding thoughts behind each of those feelings (*"I feel anxious because": I think that being passed over for promotion means that I'm going to be stuck where I am forever. "I am afraid that": I will be left behind. "I feel hurt because": I think it means that I am not good enough and they don't value me.).* Do not judge the thoughts for being illogical or unreasonable. Allow yourself to see what is quietly informing your feelings.
4. List the ways in which you desire to punish the person, place or thing (*Quitting, Slacking off, Avoiding the coworker who received your promotion*). Be honest here. It is not easy or pleasant to confront the dark side of our mind. These are not necessarily actions or behaviors that we would engage in real life, but they are the secret, dark wishes playing out in the recesses of our mind.
5. Sit with these lists for a moment and allow yourself to feel these feelings. Once you are ready to release them in order to feel better, move on to the next step.
6. Go back through your list of feelings, thoughts, and punishments in the order that they are listed and affirm your genuine willingness to let go of each one (*I willingly choose to release this feeling of..., this thought of..., this desire to punish by....*).
7. State one genuinely positive thing that you feel true love and appreciation for about both this person, place, or thing *and*

yourself. Be specific. Allow yourself to feel that love and appreciation in your heart and body. The moment or example you choose to focus on need not pertain to the issue you are forgiving. It need only pertain to you and to the subject of your forgiveness work in general. (*"I appreciate my job for offering me flexibility when I need it." Example: the time my workplace gave me extra time off because I was moving and my coworkers stepped in to cover for me. "I am thoughtful." Example: that time I surprised my sister with her favorite coffee drink at work because she was having a hard week.*)

8. State what you want from this person, place, or thing—the goal you hold for them/it (*I want my job to recognize how hard I have worked and how much I have to contribute by choosing me for this position*).
9. Affirm that you are willing and choosing to release your goal/agenda for this person, place or thing. (*Cross out the goal that you wrote down.*) Take your power back by acknowledging your capacity to choose your own feelings, thoughts, actions and behaviors.
10. Express gratitude for the forgiveness work you have done and take note of how you feel now (mentally, emotionally, physically). Jot down any new thoughts, realizations, or perspectives you may have had from going through this process.

Note: Be as specific as possible with each feeling, thought and statement of desire. The more specific you become, the clearer and easier this process becomes.

After completing these steps, allow yourself to step away from the process mentally and move on with your day. You need do nothing more. You may feel differently right away or you may not. What I have learned is that forgiveness is not usually a one trick pony. It takes practice and it grows over time. Very often, I feel a palpable internal shift during or shortly after the process, but not always. It is dependent upon the subject of your forgiveness work and the many factors and variables therein. I would encourage you not to judge yourself or the process, especially when you are just starting to practice it. Try it out with an open mind, and if it helps you, use as needed.

Being Your Own Best Friend

By now, I hope you are wise to this theme. So much of this recovery process is about rebuilding love, trust and connection *with ourselves* first, so that we can then experience those things out in the world. Complex PTSD creates a division within our own being that can leave us feeling lost, disconnected, dissociated and utterly alone. Healing that division is the work of recovery.

Learning to offer ourselves the kindness, compassion, forgiveness and love that we may have been denied by others, especially those we would have done anything to please, can be intensely challenging. For too long we have sacrificed our own needs and desires, for the sake of "peace" with others and to fulfill the needs and desires of those others. In some cases, our own happiness was simply not a priority. In other cases, we have mistaken our own happiness to be contingent upon someone else's happiness.

It is time to accept the humbling reality that *you* cannot make anyone else happy, no matter what you do. Not only is it not your responsibility, but it is simply not possible. None of us has that kind of power, despite what someone who is benefiting from our sacrifices might say. Each of us is only responsible for our own happiness. Each of us can only *choose* happiness for ourselves. Try as we might, we will never be able to make that choice for another.

Now it is time to become your own best friend. You must take that responsibility seriously. It is your job to protect yourself, advocate for yourself, provide for yourself, speak up for yourself, care for yourself, encourage yourself, speak kindly to yourself, and love yourself. It is time to love yourself like you have never been loved before. God bless the beautiful souls who join us on our path to echo and mirror these behaviors back to us, to encourage, support, love and care for us. But at the end of the day, with or without that support, we must be there for ourselves and learn to be our own biggest fans, from a place of love rather than arrogance.

If, or when, you are struggling to provide all of this goodness for yourself, I would challenge you to consider it this way:

What if your dearest, closest friend, whom you adore, were to come to you spewing hateful thoughts and judgments about herself? What if she were criticizing and blaming and tearing herself down? What would you do? What would you say to her?

Would you love her? Would you correct her? Would you remind her of all the wonderful things about her that you love so much and all the incredible things she has done? Would you comfort her? Would you be angry at how she is treating herself, your best friend?

What if you saw this person, whom you loved and adored deeply, hurting herself through destructive behaviors, ignoring her needs, neglecting herself, throwing herself away at others and rejecting your love and care for her? What would you do? What would you say to her?

Now remember: You *are* her. Approach and care for yourself as you would the person you love most in this world. You have so much compassion for others, so much love and kindness and goodness to offer to this world. It leaks out of you because it is in the essence of who you are. It is time to take all of that goodness and direct it towards yourself, at last. You have so much to give. Once you do this, you will be amazed to discover just how much more you have to offer the world than you ever knew before.

Lay that Baggage Down

Have you ever seen the movie *Goodwill Hunting?* If so, you'll probably remember that iconic scene of emotional breakthrough between Matt Damon's character and the therapist character played by Robin Williams. If not, I'll describe it briefly here. Williams looks Damon in the eye and says, "It's not your fault." Williams is referring to the abuse Damon endured as a child. "It's not your fault" he repeats, genuinely and patiently. Williams continues to repeat this statement as we witness Damon have a cascade of emotional reactions from flippancy to anger to full emotional breakdown. Williams persists, asserting to Damon "It's not your fault," until he reaches that ooey-gooey painful center of internalized blame and shame.

Just as with Damon's character, it is not *your* fault. Take time to sit with this. Take time to be honest with yourself about the reactions that come up. Take time to feel the absolutely abhorrent feelings buried deep beneath the surface and to investigate the thoughts attached to those feelings. Write it out. Cry it out. Scream it out. Dance it out. Punch it out. Whatever comes up, let it out of you in whatever *safe* way it wants or needs to come out. Let it come up, let it flow out and let it go.

It is also not *your* fault.

No matter what you were told. No matter what you did to cope. No matter what you had to do to survive. No matter what you endured in the process. The abuse that occurred, the pain that you endured, the trauma that you survived *was not your fault*. You did not deserve it. No matter what they said. No matter what they did. No matter how they tried to convince you that there was something wrong with *you*—you did not deserve the treatment that you received.

Forgive yourself. Embrace yourself. Accept yourself.

You used the resources at your disposal to survive that situation. You did the very best you could with what you had at the time. You did the very best you could with what you *knew* at the time. In the words of the inimitable Maya Angelou, "Do the best you can until you know better. Then when you know better, do better." When you knew better, or had more, you did better and you did more.

You were not perfect. You are still not perfect. There are things you wish you had done differently. Maybe there are things you wish you could do better now. Ask yourself: Am I doing the best I am capable of in each and every moment? If I had been capable of doing more, or doing better, at that time, wouldn't I have?

Forgive yourself.

Love yourself.

Extend compassion, understanding and grace to yourself. Appreciate yourself for all you have done, all you have come through and all you are committed to still doing for yourself and your healing. Commit to a daily diet of self-love.

You are doing your best. That is all anyone can ask. It is all you need to ask of yourself. Appreciate yourself for your commitment to grow, heal, improve and make your ten-square-feet of space in this world as beautiful as possible.

Do not downplay the significance of doing this work. Saving yourself is akin to saving the world. Your mind and heart are the only thing that you have absolute and total control over in this life. If each one of us took full responsibility for saving ourselves, would not the whole world then be saved as well?

Please be gentle with yourself as you do this work. Remember, there is no one-and-done technique. It is a process and one in which we will engage for the rest of our lives if we wish to grow. Therefore, there is no perfection to reach or final destination at which to arrive. It is a *journey,* and as we know better, we do better, and the journey continues....

Just like that beautiful spiral sequence that reappears throughout our natural world, we seemingly return to where we started, and yet somehow, at a new place. With each bit of work and healing we do, we reach down to find a new layer beneath. As we spiral through this process, we eventually discover that we have laid a solid foundation of love onto which we can confidently build our new lives. Be patient. Be good to yourself. Be proud of yourself. And most of all, *keep going.*

About the Author

Christina Cummings has dedicated over twenty years to writing and reflecting on the complexities of the human condition. Her work delves deeply into what makes life meaningful, drawing from both personal experience and thoughtful observation.

"The Journey Back to Self" marks Christina's debut as an author. This book is a testament to her unwavering commitment to uncovering beauty and goodness, even in the midst of adversity. The inspiration for her writing stems from her determined pursuit of hope and positivity regardless of the challenges she has faced.

Christina's personal journey includes surviving a childhood shaped by high control religion and, later, enduring cultic and narcissistic abuse as an adult. She spent fourteen years as a member of a therapy-based high control group, experiences that profoundly influenced her perspective on life and healing.

Through her writing and lived experiences, Christina Cummings finds purpose in transforming life's darkest moments into sources of goodness. Her story encourages others to seek hope and create positive change, even when faced with hardship.

You can connect with me on:

https://christinamcummings.com

www.ingramcontent.com/pod-product-compliance
Lightning Source LLC
Chambersburg PA
CBHW070915130626
46555CB00001B/141

* 9 7 9 8 9 9 3 6 4 1 2 0 1 *